P9-CCK-268

How Great Decisions Get Made

10 Easy Steps for Reaching Agreement on Even the Toughest Issues

Don Maruska

Foreword by Margaret J. Wheatley

AMACOM

American Management Association
New York • Atlanta • Brussels • Chicago • Mexico City
San Francisco • Shanghai • Tokyo • Toronto • Washington, D. C.

Special discounts on bulk quantities of AMACOM books are available to corporations, professional associations, and other organizations. For details, contact Special Sales Department, AMACOM, a division of American Management Association, 1601 Broadway, New York, NY 10019.
Tel.: 212-903-8316. Fax: 212-903-8083.
Web site: www.amacombooks.org

This publication is designed to provide accurate and authoritative information in regard to the subject matter covered. It is sold with the understanding that the publisher is not engaged in rendering legal, accounting, or other professional service. If legal advice or other expert assistance is required, the services of a competent professional person should be sought.

Library of Congress Cataloging-in-Publication Data

Maruska, Don.
How great decisions get made : 10 easy steps for reaching agreement on even the toughest issues / Don Maruska. — 1st ed.
p. cm.
Includes bibliographical references.
ISBN 0-8144-0793-5
1. Group decision making. I. Title.

HD30.23.M375 2003
658.4'036—dc21 2003010065

© 2004 Don Maruska
All rights reserved.
Printed in the United States of America.

Illustrations on pp. 67 and 77 by Andrew Ellul.

This publication may not be reproduced, stored in a retrieval system, or transmitted in whole or in part, in any form or by any means, electronic, mechanical, photocopying, recording, or otherwise, without the prior written permission of AMACOM, a division of American Management Association, 1601 Broadway, New York, NY 10019.

Printing number

10 9 8 7 6 5 4 3 2 1

This book is dedicated to Art for inspiring me and Liz and Katy for encouraging me.

Contents

Foreword

I no longer meet people who look forward to going to work meetings. Or public hearings. Or school board meetings. Or any session where decisions need to be made. We don't want to be at these meetings because we know exactly what will happen. People will either overparticipate or sit there bored. Those who talk will become progressively louder and more emotional. One or two people will monopolize the process and try to ramrod through their agenda, while everyone else gets angry at their tactics. We won't feel listened to; we won't believe that anyone understands our position. And nothing will get done—the problem that called us together, that each of us cares about, will not be resolved. If a decision gets made, it will not represent us, and our relationships will be more fractured at the meeting's end than when we started.

In the past few years, I've watched the disintegration of decision-making processes in organizations, communities, and families. I've observed how difficult it is for people to work together, how we no longer want to work together, and how frustrated we all are that no one seems capable of good decision making. How did we get into this sorry mess? When and why did it become so difficult to work together well? Was there ever a time when we left meetings feeling good about the quality of our decision making, when we enjoyed working together, when we looked forward to the next time we could think and dream together?

Don Maruska knows how to create positive, productive meetings and successful decisions in today's fractured and exhausted environment. His well-tested process makes it possible to reach high-quality decisions based on accessing everyone's good thinking and greatest hopes. He has found the means to bring out people's best qualities—their intelligence, their caring, their commitment. His ten-step process reaches back in time to another tradition—that of spiritual discernment—that precedes our current flawed methods. This process is more firmly rooted in a deep understanding of human motivation and the conditions that bring out our best qualities.

Several years ago, Marvin Weisbord, one of the wisest consultants I know, taught a great principle. After many years of working in organizations, he commented: "I used to ask 'What's wrong and how can we fix it?' Then I realized that the right question is 'What's possible and who cares?' " Marvin's comment changed my work in profound ways. I, like so many others, had been taught to ask "What's wrong? What's the problem?" The only process I knew was to flesh out the problem and to do that by asking a team of people to define the issues more fully. I would stand at a flip chart and write down everyone's comments. Soon the paper would be filled with depressing information. People would stare at the paper and sink into their seats, overwhelmed and exhausted by the dimensions of the problem.

Then we would enter into analysis. We would look for clusters of issues, themes, categories. After we lumped things together, we would prioritize them. Then we'd assign people or small groups to work on each priority. People would leave the meeting to go work on their part of the problem, often grateful just to get out of the room and stop breathing the depressing air of analysis. At the next meeting, people might have worked on their issue, or they might not have. But at this meeting, we only had energy for ending the torture. Any action would feel better than delving deeper into the problem. People wanted to get out of the room, and the easiest ticket out was to agree to do something, even if the action made no real sense.

I expect that you've participated in more than one of these problem-solving meetings. As much as we resent them, we haven't known how to change them, because we've been convinced that the only way to solve a problem is to analyze it to death. Yet Don has learned the same lesson as Weisbord. Ask: "What's possible?" Stay away from "What's wrong?" As Don advises, work from hope, not from fear. Think of yourself as an "agent of hope." Call people together to invoke their hopefulness, not their fear.

I'm not surprised that Don's approach has centuries-old roots. It's just in recent times that we've used purely analytic processes, where numbers are the only honored information. We've created nice, neat, linear processes, assembling data into columns and rows, describing step-by-step how plans will unfold, and reducing complex issues to simple formulas. We haven't noticed that these reductionist processes also reduce us. They exclude our greatest human capacities—our multiple intelligences, our feelings, our creativity. Yet it is only these capacities that make it possible to deal with life in all its complexity and fullness.

It takes visionaries like Don to liberate us from these deeply dissatisfying processes. His process isn't a new fad piled on top of existing ones. It is a restoration of what has worked through time for people everywhere. Don has opened an ancient door that we can step through to find the solutions we need, approaches developed by people who weren't living inside modern-day organizations. This book shows how to put these understandings into practice and how to overcome the obstacles in organizational life that stand in the way.

There are several elements to this ten-step process that I know to be true for all human beings, independent of culture or location.

The first element is that people need to be included in issues and decisions that affect them. Very few humans are content to have decisions made for them. Every time we go to a meeting, even when we know it will be a frustrating session, we're acting from this need. We need to be included.

Second, we never know who might have the information that will make a difference, that will provide the insights necessary to solve a problem. Everyone is an expert about something, and processes that make it possible for people to speak from their unique expertise always lead to more intelligent decisions.

Third, people need to feel respected. This is a fundamental

human need, no matter how poor or oppressed or excluded we've been in our lives. Any process that truly welcomes people in and respects them for their experience will succeed.

Fourth, listening is the most powerful process we have available. As we listen to each other, we move closer together. Our relationships improve considerably. And people who feel listened to become good listeners. As we listen to each other, we learn how differently each of us experiences the world. Those different perceptions allow us to create a richer picture of what's going on. We move off of our narrow positions and become more sensitive to the complexity of life. We become better thinkers, and also better colleagues.

Fifth, people want to be together. We are happiest when we can work well together. It is antithetical to human nature to be alone—we are a species that has always worked in groups. Sometimes this is difficult to believe, especially at this time of broken relationships and demoralizing group processes. But the most fundamental aspect of being human is our capacity to love.

And finally, it is hope that calls us into our creativity. We love to feel that we can make a difference in our world—that by contributing our caring and our ideas, we will make something possible. We are by nature a meaning-seeking species, and we find meaning in hoping that we can make the world better for our children. We are intent on creating a future that is better than the present. This hope is not dependent on circumstances, but is a quality of the human spirit.

As you read this book and experiment with this process, I encourage you to see if what I've just described becomes true in your own experience. You're about to engage in a wonderful discovery of what it feels like for people to work together to find true solutions. Enjoy the discovery.

—Margaret J. Wheatley
Author of *Leadership and the New Science*, *A Simpler Way*, and *Turning to One Another: Simple Conversations to Restore Hope*

Acknowledgments

I am especially thankful to my wife Liz and daughter Katy for their support throughout the ten years during which I developed and applied the process outlined in this book. Although I've focused on businesses, government, and community organizations externally, we've been making our own great decisions in our home laboratory.

Art Stevens generously shared the spiritual traditions of this process with me. He also encouraged my efforts to develop it for a wide range of secular applications.

Dozens of client organizations and thousands of people gave me the opportunity to help them resolve tough issues and, most important, to learn with them and hone the concepts and procedures. I particularly appreciate the early support from Bill Statler, John Dunn, John Moss, Gary Henderson, Ken Hampian, and Bill and Ed Thoma. Many others followed, including Mike and Myra Gilfix, Steve Goschke, Bob Fredianelli, Bill Hall, Pam Martens, Jim Brabeck, Lauren Brown, Mary Bradley, Barbara Underwood, Steve Ladd, Ron Fellows, Mike Pool, Linda Hansen, Greg Haas, Karen Wood, Kara Blakeslee, Myron Nalepa, Chuck Cova, Ann Foxworthy, Scott Burns, and a much longer list.

Treasured friends and colleagues read drafts, offered key perspectives, and provided moral support. They include John Steinhart, Jim Thompson, Dean Michelson, Roger Sattler, Betty Kaufman, Ned Trainor, John Ashbaugh, Allen Minker, and Dick Armfield.

Several of my professors at Stanford Business School particularly inspired my thinking. Michael Ray's insightful creativity concepts and encouragement have nourished me for over two decades. Similarly, Jim March offered perspectives on leadership and organizations that have stood the test of time.

I'm thankful for Paul Brest, who as dean of Stanford Law School took an interest in this approach to decision making. I appreciated the early opportunity to guest-lecture on the topic.

Meg Wheatley's path-finding work on self-organizing systems and the need to reclaim conversation to solve issues added insights and inspiration for my efforts. I'm honored that she chose to share her thoughts in the foreword to this book.

Amid all of this activity, Judy Stevens, Stu Schlegel, Benedict Reid, and Mary-Elizabeth Pratt Horsley helped me keep my spiritual center. In addition, over the past decade, Thomas Leonard, Jeff Raim, and Shirley Anderson coached me on the business and personal sides of life. Their distinctive abilities to see the truth and share it with deep compassion and encouragement guided me to blaze my trail and follow it.

In terms of writing the book, many people aided me. I particularly appreciate the early interest that Silas Lyons took in my work that led to my "Business Success" column published through the Knight-Ridder Business Wire. The enthusiastic response from readers in the United States, Europe, and Asia demonstrated the market for this book. Sandy Duerr, Larry Mauter, Raven Railey, and Katherine Rowlands have provided continuing support.

Bill Blundell generously read my early drafts. He provided the critical advice to "show not tell" the readers. Jude Long and her talented and friendly library staff provided valuable service and encouragement. Elaine Borden kept my office running smoothly. Susan Suffes and Carol Whiteley helped shape the manuscript with very useful editing. My agent, Carol Susan Roth, championed the message and adeptly guided me through the publishing process with unwavering commitment. Adrienne Hickey at AMACOM Books immediately understood and appreciated this book's themes.

Early in my life, my mother instilled an abiding commitment to excel and spent countless hours helping me learn how to write. My father modeled the listening to others and working together that this book espouses. My brother kept me from taking myself too seriously and demonstrated living one's hopes.

Finally, I give thanks for the divine spirit that I see alive in even the toughest issues. My deepest hope is that this book and your use of it will honor that inspiration.

Introduction

> Every time our management team meets, I steel myself for a big battle over any important issue. Of course, we've tried to create trust and a better spirit of cooperation. I can't tell you how many retreats we've been to and how many rope courses we've taken, but nothing works. Everyone has a particular way of doing things and no one wants to change. I really enjoy my work, but the way decisions are made around here is killing me.

Sound familiar? From the boardroom to the conference room to city hall, members of teams everywhere find it difficult, if not impossible, to resolve tough issues together. Instead of cooperation and encouragement they face

- Battling egos
- Conflicting styles
- Lack of commitment and follow-through
- Office politics
- Knee-jerk actions
- Seemingly irreconcilable differences
- An atmosphere of defeatism
- A legacy of distrust

Despite the advances of technology and the desire to build business relationships, many businesses and organizations have yet to find a positive, results-oriented process for reaching agreement as a team.

Why is this the case? It's because most group members operate out of fear: fear that their team won't succeed, that other members will take all the credit for an idea, or that their contributions won't be acknowledged. Most of all, they fear that they'll get less than someone else.

That fear creates scarcity. Just think back to the gasoline shortages of the early 1970s. Long lines snaked behind gas stations all over the United States because citizens feared that the oil embargo would mean empty gas tanks. Drivers filled up their tanks more often, which drained pumps faster and created the shortages that were feared. Instead of thinking of the interests of everyone, people thought only of their own interests. They ignored the opportunity to conserve supplies and have a positive effect on the greater community.

Jockeying for influence or position in organizational teams, rather than working together, creates scarcity in the same way. When participants continually strive for personal recognition and reward at the expense of others, everyone becomes conditioned to expect less. That expectation becomes self-perpetuating.

The idea of scarcity *is* frightening. It represents emotional hunger, physical stress, and spiritual numbness. And, of course, it cultivates an atmosphere in which little can be done as a team because the mind-set is that there won't be enough to go around. Then struggle becomes the norm, because every person is in it for him- or herself. People jump to conclusions and don't bother to investigate other people's intentions. The situation becomes hopeless, as do all similar situations that follow.

Although this may seem like an insurmountable problem, in reality it's not. There *is* a way for people to work together and make effective decisions—especially in tough circumstances. The key is to work from hopes instead of fears.

HOPES GET RESULTS

Hopes are the last thing that most groups making a decision seem to have—there are plenty of fears and frustrations, but generally no hopes. Hopes, however, are essential for productive teamwork and effective decision making and for achieving the outcomes we want. That's because hopes break through self-imposed limitations and provide the foundation for wide-ranging results. How do they do this? By overriding the primal fear of scarcity and by embracing the possibility of more abundant, more fulfilling alternatives.

Hopes also enable teams to work smart and support one another. This "intelligent teamwork" allows them to

- Embrace a worldview that encourages joining together to create better results
- Shift their attention from the stale, ineffective "What should we do?" approach to the fresh, results-producing "How can we achieve what we really want?" approach
- Tap into who they are, which gives their work added meaning and helps them define and focus on their goals

Intelligent teamwork can cement a group during decision making, rather than pull it apart. In more than ten years of experience in using the process with dozens of large companies as well as embattled communities and small businesses with big problems, I've seen it enable all kinds of groups to solve all kinds of problems together. I've also seen how it brings out the best in people—without requiring them to go through a long, drawn-out process of "personal development."

My enthusiasm for intelligent teamwork and my development of the ten-step process detailed here came about the hard way. In the early 1990s I helped found a biotech company with two partners. We wanted to work together; we had mutual respect and supported each other through the endless hours we dedicated to making a medical breakthrough.

Soon, though, the company needed a multi-million-dollar infusion of capital. Unfortunately, the timing was lousy. The biotech sector was in a severe down cycle, and the few venture investors who expressed interest wanted to control our business. What had started out as a cooperative, mutually encouraging, and productive working relationship turned into a debilitating association seething with conflict and frustration. The decision-making processes we used didn't work. All three founders—myself included—as well as the investors, fought for control. In the midst of the turmoil, I—the CEO—was squeezed out.

But that wasn't all. When my work situation splintered, my relationship with my wife suffered, too. With demanding business lives and a young child to care for and enjoy, the tension between us hit the critical mark. Everyday topics became hot-button issues. It didn't matter whether we were deciding who would pick up our daughter from preschool or how we should spend our money. Tempers flared and no solution seemed right.

Thankfully, and just in time, we discovered a new way to take action together.

A BETTER WAY TO WORK AS A TEAM

The discovery came from an unexpected source: an Episcopal priest and modern-day spiritual guide named Art Stevens. For several years, Art had preached and conducted workshops on an ancient but radical way of understanding and pursuing hopes. When I attended one of Art's workshops, he told me about the power of hopes and showed me the difference between hopes and expectations.

Expectations—what you or others think about how things *should* be—have nothing to do with what you truly desire. I learned that hopes are what we really want when we are honest with ourselves and others. Art told me that in order to find a way to move ahead we need to determine what we really want, what's truly important to us.

When I asked myself what I really wanted, I had to stop and look inside myself, rather than concentrate on all that was going on around me. When I gave myself that time, I realized that my hopes involved not only me but also my family. So my wife and I developed a set of hopes together. These hopes included aspirations such as being in balance with ourselves, contributing to and supporting a positive spirit of community, sustaining financial flexibility, being healthy and happy, finding peace in what we feel called to do, and living abundantly amid uncertainty.

When I outlined our hopes to Art, he said, "Congratulations. Articulating your hopes is the first step to living them." Then he offered a straightforward path for putting hopes into action.

With nothing left to lose, my wife and I tried the process. We stopped second-guessing each other and discovered that we could really hear one another and the stirrings of a common spirit within us. To our surprise, we found agreement in our answers even though we differed greatly in our reasons and thinking. We stopped trying to convince each other that our own point of view was correct and moved on with our decisions.

Sooner than either of us expected, we resolved long-standing conflicts and settled our differences. Best of all, we improved our relationship, which continues to thrive.

That transformation encouraged another one. I realized that if the hopes-based method cleared the air for my wife and me and helped us to make thoughtful, useful decisions, the same basic technique could apply to business.

The thought was so compelling that I took a sabbatical from my entrepreneurial endeavors to develop a business-oriented process. Over time I developed a ten-step approach that remained faithful to the central elements of inclusiveness and shared hopes yet applied to all types of relationships and all types of issues. I went on to help others use the process to be successful in their organizations. I sought the toughest of tough issues and the most divisive group situations and helped people discover great solutions and new and exciting ways to work together.

As an entrepreneur, I focus on things that work and provide a big return for the effort. In over three decades as a consultant, CEO, and venture investor in successful companies, this ten-step process is the best way I've found for resolving tough issues. I want you to enjoy its benefits.

TEN EASY STEPS FOR REACHING AGREEMENTS TOGETHER

Just what are the ten steps that get such amazing results? The second part of this book explains them thoroughly, but in brief they are as follows:

1. Enlist everyone.
2. Discover your shared hopes.
3. Uncover the real issues.
4. Identify all options.
5. Gather the right information.
6. Get everything on the table.
7. Write down choices that support your shared hopes.
8. Map the solutions.
9. Look ahead.
10. Stay charged up.

Each step provides insight into an issue as well as problem-solving techniques. But it's *how* the steps work together that brings out the best in participants and produces extraordinary, sustainable results. Together, the steps have benefited a wide range of organizations, from Fortune 500 companies to growing businesses to government agencies to community nonprofits. As you read, you'll learn how each step connects with and advances the next, and in Strategy #1 in Part 3 you'll discover how all the steps can come together for quick results on specific issues.

To show you how the process works, I've included wide-ranging examples and illustrations based upon my experiences with dozens of organizations and thousands of people during more than a decade of work with teams and groups facing some of the toughest issues of their lives. (I've changed the names and organizational details so that you can learn from them without putting the particular people involved on the spot or breaching confidential relationships.) These stories give you a bird's-eye view of how people applied the process and illustrations for you to visualize ways to use it. I hope they inspire you to apply the steps and strategies in your own work and activities.

This book focuses mainly on business issues, but the process works equally well with issues you face in every part of your life. Indeed, that's one of the process's distinctive benefits. You can practice it in any aspect of your work, community, or home life and benefit from the experience in the others. No matter what your tough issue is, the process will help you learn how to make your own great decisions.

Even if you don't face a tough issue now, following these steps can enhance your life. For example, you can positively change the tenor of any discussion by asking the powerful questions in Step #2: "What are your hopes about this [topic]?" and "Why are they important to you?" Step #6 shows you how to discuss even the most controversial issue without a single minute of divisive debate. Similarly, each of the other steps contains nuggets you can put into practice immediately to improve your daily interactions.

Don't let obstacles keep you and your group from making

progress. Some people despair that they lack time or they aren't in charge. Part 3 identifies six common obstacles and gives you strategies to handle them quickly and painlessly. For example, the 30-Minute Miracle technique, detailed in Strategy #1, quick-starts the agreement process when time is short, letting you work not only smarter but faster. Persuasive techniques in Strategy #2 enable even the powerless to guide fractious groups to effective solutions. You can make a difference.

THE NUMBERS REVEAL HUGE OPPORTUNITIES

If you're frustrated with trying to make important decisions and get results together, you're not alone. A few years ago, Stanford Business School asked an array of alumni to talk about what they found difficult in their jobs and where better training would be desirable. These leaders, with many years of experience in different sectors of the economy, most frequently cited the need for more effective ways to reach agreement and get results with diverse groups of people. The organizational dynamics of bringing people together on major projects, new mergers, or tough community issues frustrated them more than any of the technical challenges in their jobs. With increasing diversity in the workplace, more multinational businesses, and the advent of virtual teams, the challenges mount.

In an effort to explore typical decision-making practices and the frustrations people have with them, I conducted an informal survey of thirty-six organizations. It involved middle managers from a sample of manufacturing firms, service businesses, and government and educational organizations of various sizes. I focused on middle managers because they generally exhibit a healthy level of candor and are in a position to see up, down, and sideways in their organizations. Fewer than 10 percent of those organizations had discovered and consistently applied preactices like those in the ten-step process. (See

Appendix A for the survey, which you can take for your own organization.)

While the gap between typical decision-making practices and the ten-step process is huge, the effort to bridge it is not. As you'll read, organizations have followed the process and resolved the toughest of issues in as little as an afternoon's time. So, you can see results quickly. Sustaining these results and building capacity within your organization to facilitate future sessions takes further commitment. The great thing is that early successes build interest and momentum to sustain these practices.

Bottom line, the ten-step process serves huge unmet needs, yields big improvements in performance, and offers easy ways to get started and to continue your success.

ON YOUR WAY TO A WORLD OF POSSIBILITIES

If you've been bogged down in divisive and unproductive debates, just imagine what it would be like if your team members' philosophy was "We can do this together." Consider what could be accomplished if your group concluded, "Even if we don't have the solution right now, we'll find what works for us and serves everybody's needs." Think about what could happen if your coworkers or the members of your community had energy and resilience and were willing to listen to one another with patience and respect, if they were not only open to new ideas and opportunities, but also excited by them. Wouldn't it be wonderful to be part of an organization or community that works that way?

It *is* possible for teams to solve tough issues together and get great results. By using the easy approach that follows, your team can do it, too.

BE AN AGENT OF HOPE

While many people manage their teams with fear and by following personal agendas, you can choose to pursue hopes and discover opportunities for more positive, beneficial outcomes. I call people who pursue outstanding results in this way *agents of hope.* These leaders tap the positive spirit within them and their team, rather than their own narrow expectations, to guide their work and their lives. They are not wishful thinkers. Rather, they are doers focused upon understanding the deepest aspirations within a group and acting to realize them.

The ten steps and the six strategies in this book will help you become an agent of hope. There is a "Be an Agent of Hope" box at the end of Part 1 and at the end of each of the steps and strategies. The epilogue, "Be an Agent of Hope in a Fearful World" pulls these themes together and underscores how they enhance results.

PART 1

Making Great Decisions

Of all the forces that make for a better world, none is so indispensable, none so powerful, as hope.
—Charles Sawyer

Great decisions bring out the best in people and galvanize them to achieve great results together. Great decisions also attract the interest, energy, and resources that members of any team or group effort need to implement them. What's more, great decisions resolve tough issues with flexible solutions that adapt to changing conditions.

Unfortunately, too few great decisions, or even good decisions, get made. Instead, tough issues fester. Businesses fall short of their potential. Communities struggle. Everyone suffers.

Why? Call it the irony of technology. Although communication hardware has multiplied our ability to transmit information, "human software"—our ability to use information to decide issues together—doesn't work nearly as well. Anyone can send a stinging e-mail to everyone they know in seconds. But when they need to decide a tough issue constructively, many people don't even know how to begin.

Typical decision-making processes set people against each other.

When groups face tough issues, even people with the best of intentions can find themselves locked in divisive and destructive debates. Instead of energizing people to work as a team, most decision-making practices only work to polarize them. This slows down the wheels of progress, betrays organizational values, and undermines results. Such traditional approaches waste time and sap a group's energy and spirit.

The good news is that it doesn't have to be that way. The process detailed in this book is transforming. When you learn how to make great decisions together, your team members will connect with each other through their deepest hopes and aspirations. This in turn will help them discover ways to turn their hopes into concrete action and achieve lasting results.

FEAR UNDERMINES DECISION MAKING

Why do typical decision processes produce ineffective and lackluster results? The answer, as mentioned in the introduction, is fear. Hardly anyone is immune to the contagion of fear that can envelop a tough issue. Even the best and the brightest of us succumb to it. Take, for example, a research and development (R&D) group at a Fortune 500 company.

"I'm under the gun here," Tim, the manager, said. "I need to get great results from my group and I need them now. Our company has searched the planet to hire the best people. We employ the leading software programmers, psychologists, and designers, and we have a lofty purpose—to make computers dramatically easier for people to use. I've got an open checkbook to buy what we need and access to a world-class advisory board. But my group members can't even agree on which couch to put in our lounge."

Tim had the horses, but they weren't pulling together. He needed his workers to collaborate to create an integrated set of tools to incorporate into millions of computers, but different members of his team favored different approaches, and each had invested significant time and effort to develop projects based on personal software choices. Because they couldn't decide issues together, they went off on their own to concentrate on their separate projects. Not surprisingly, they weren't able to build on each other's work.

Tim worried about what to do. He didn't want to take an authoritarian stance and squelch individual creativity. Yet the team wasn't working together. He needed a way to encourage everyone's input *and* get a durable decision that would motivate group members to work together.

But fear gripped Tim's group. Though there was an abundance of resources, each group member was afraid that there wouldn't be enough time, money, and recognition (especially recognition) to go around. Nobody could think beyond protecting his or her own agenda and way of doing things.

The fear that plagued Tim's group plagues all kinds of organizations and groups of people who are trying to decide issues together. Even in an environment of abundance, fear can cause people to see scarcity. And once fear takes hold, all decision making (even on mundane issues such as which couch to put in the lounge) becomes difficult.

> "No passion so effectually robs the mind of all its powers of acting and reasoning as fear."
>
> —Edmund Burke

The Legacy of Fear

The underpinnings of fear and scarcity lie deep within our culture. For example, *business economics* is defined as the study of how people choose to employ scarce resources. Classic definitions of government describe the process of allocating limited resources—who gets which slice of a very small pie.

Unfortunately, the primary reason that fear-driven group dynamics are so pervasive is that at some level they get results. Managers who win at office politics by spreading fear feel vindicated, especially when they advance in their organizations. So why should they change tactics that work for them? Employees of start-ups, afraid that they'll run out of money or that a major competitor will crush them, work extremely long hours, and often their on-the-edge performance gets good results.

The fact is that, although fear can provide near-term benefits, those benefits usually come at the cost of long-term consequences. Fear-induced behavior marginalizes and discourages employees who lose out in power struggles. Eventually these people stop offering their new ideas and voicing their concerns, because they fear they'll just be shot down. And the problem isn't just inside the organiza-

FEARS GET IN THE WAY

Fears plague organizations by setting up a system of negative behaviors and responses that rarely vary. This system includes:

Negative thoughts: What you want is scarce.

Troubled feelings: There won't be enough to go around. You can never get enough.

Disruptive behavior: People become abrupt, short-tempered, and self-protective.

Frayed relationships: Participants become suspicious of one another. Cooperation declines.

tion. Fear can also cause missed opportunities to forge collaborations with suppliers or competitors and build new markets.

As opportunities—and risks—become greater, the potential for fears to overtake an organization's decision-making dynamics mounts. When difficult circumstances arise or big financial interests are at stake, groups clamp down, becoming less open to fresh insights or unconventional thinking. The quest for control overrides the need for inclusion and respect, and all that's wanted are preconceived results.

Fears Create Scarcity

Examples abound of what happens when fears go unchecked. Listen to Greg, a manager responsible for municipal water supplies. "All of our critical projects, where we desperately need to work together, are locked up in fears," he lamented. "One city council is afraid that their city will run out of water. In that same community, others fear that new water resources will stimulate undesired growth. People in nearby areas with extra water supplies dread that they will lose those resources. Put representatives from all these places in a room and guess what happens? Nothing of value. Each person representing a particular group seeks to control the agenda and fulfill the objectives of that group. I understand the reason—running out of water is a very serious matter—but no one thinks about any concern other than his or her own. The truth is, there is plenty of water to go around, but all of the parties are so afraid of scarcity that they can't acknowledge it. How can they manage the problem when fear narrows their vision?"

Similarly, fear thwarts effective decision making and teamwork in other settings. Whether it's vying for the corner office or trying to push an agenda in a self-serving direction, employees who want to win or be in control at the expense of their colleagues propel their organizations into fear-filled dynamics. Their worries that there won't be enough to go around drive them to get their own needs for recognition and reward met first.

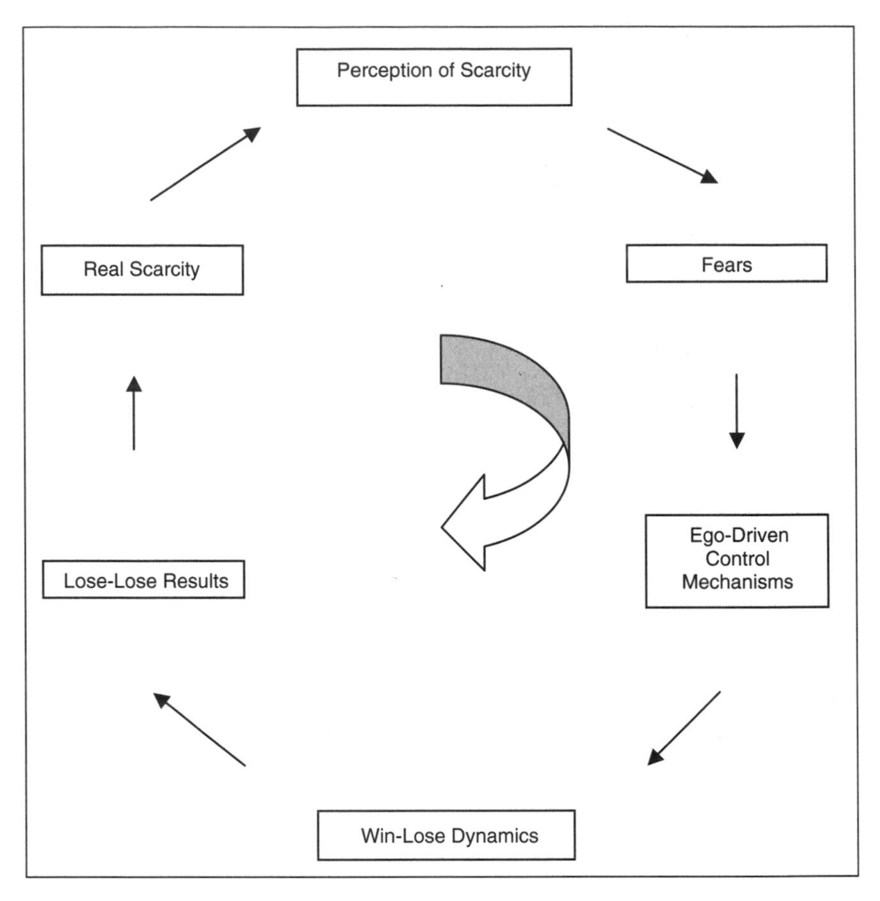

FIGURE 1 The cycle of fear and scarcity.

Fear of not getting enough stimulates ego-driven control mechanisms. This prompts win-lose dynamics, a contest of wills. Who will prevail and get the recognition, resources, and rewards? Who will lose out? In time, lose-lose dynamics become the norm. People who have lost power plot how to regain it. Those in control fear that someone will overtake them. These factions create the conditions for the very scarcity they feared in the first place. (See Figure 1.)

A mind-set of scarcity limits what people can accomplish. Even more dramatically, it restricts their enjoyment of what they do and create. Instead of a positive, joyful environment, the world becomes a fear-filled place.

Fueled by adrenaline from instinctive reactions to fear-filled situations, the cycle of fear and scarcity goes on. Eventually, frustration and exhaustion result in burnout, but by then the damage has been done. The people involved withdraw, needing time to recover so they can address the issue more constructively. Sometimes an infusion of new people and new energy is required to move forward. In any case, the toll is high.

Fears Provoke Decision-Making Problems

The cycle of fear shuts down decision making in ten different ways:

1. *People get left out of the decision-making process.* "They'll be disruptive" and "We don't have time to include them" typify the mind-set. Excluding people, however, undermines the breadth of involvement and support needed for truly creative solutions and successful implementation.

2. *Participants lose sight of what they really want.* Expectations obscure participants' true hopes and their potential to work together. Participants focus on their own slice of the pie and how big it is relative to everyone else's rather than figuring out how to make the pie bigger for the benefit of all.

3. *The real issues get ignored or overlooked.* The feverish quest for control clouds the picture and distracts attention from what's really important. Participants hide their agendas for fear of "showing their hand." Issues become more difficult to resolve because people don't talk about what is really in play.

4. *Participants miss important options.* They jump on the first idea or defend their own, which keeps them from seeing other

choices. Fears short-circuit the deeper integration of information and creative connections needed for innovation.

5. *Information gathering is biased and inefficient.* Advocates only get information to support their own positions or refute others'. There are no guiding principles for focused and balanced inquiry. Some people study issues to excess because they don't know what they're looking for or they fear the consequences of making a choice.

6. *Participants become personally attached to preset positions or expectations.* They're less able to receive new information and change their viewpoints. They ignore or reject information that could lead them to better results. In their minds, the risk of showing tentativeness or losing face overrides the need to find the best path.

7. *Someone or some group drives the decision with a personal agenda.* With self-protection as the first priority, participants lose sight of the bigger picture. The quest for personal victory overshadows the potential of win-win solutions.

8. *All the choices and areas for potential agreement and opportunities aren't explored.* Majority or authoritarian rule often decides the path. Participants miss seeing the total solution and ways to fashion improved results.

9. *Decisions don't stick.* Both winners and losers make poor learners. Winners revel in self-congratulation. Defeated or excluded people rally to reverse the decision. In both cases, they lack the openess necessary to perceive changes promptly and respond productively.

10. *Dissension builds.* As difficulties mount, fears increase. Dissatisfaction spills over into other issues. Soon, even mundane issues become difficult to decide. The fear spiral takes hold.

The ten-step process provides solutions for each of these problems.

The Faces of Fear

Where decision making is concerned, participants foment fear in many different ways. Some do it by fighting. Others do it by being completely nonconfrontational.

The Fighters

Steve is what's known as a *Gladiator,* someone who is willing to "fight to the death." Attacking others—often personally—is the way he spreads fear and prevails.

Steve relishes the power he wields in a high-tech start-up. As finance director and self-appointed protector of investors' assets, he weighs in on many marketing and production issues and exerts heavy influence over the board of directors.

When other staff members bring up new product ideas, they steel themselves in anticipation of Steve's blistering attacks and take-no-prisoners attitude. Steve does not disappoint. Within seconds, he points out the financial shortcomings of almost any idea. His unyielding approach, fueled by financial data, detailed spreadsheets, and bankers' ratios, destroys many promising ideas. Steve feels that he is the most qualified person to make decisions, so why should he listen to anyone else?

The Gladiator is a well-known, frequently encountered fighter. But there are five additional types of fighters:

The Boss. Because this person holds power or is in a position of authority, he or she makes all the decisions. Employees automatically go along with (but perhaps secretly resist) the company line.

The Debater. This employee becomes pitted against another Debater with an opposing view. Arguments continue until one side weakens or the bonds between the two fray and finally break.

The Majority Ruler. This polite form of the Gladiator wreaks havoc by saying, "Let's take a vote and let the majority rule."

Even in landslides, 40 percent or more of the people involved are frustrated with the decision.

The Briber. This bargainer cajoles, "Give me what I want on *this,* and I'll support you on *that.*"

The Blackmailer. True to the name, this person threatens, "If I don't get my way, I'll [hurt you in some way]." Not surprisingly, dealing with a Blackmailer precludes either rational discussion or cooperative action.

Within the volatile fight group, the underlying assumption is that, after the bloody battle of wits is over, the truth will triumph. Sometimes the fight is covered with a thin coat of civil behavior so it can be called a debate. Other times it follows dramatic courtroom-type procedures so that participants can either argue or defend their positions. Sometimes shouting matches break out. But however the fight takes place, organizations that allow this behavior to continue are treating their people worse than they treat their production equipment. After all, intelligent businesspeople don't pit one machine against another to see which can destroy the other and believe that any good will come of it. Yet, many organizations position one person or one division against another in a twisted version of Darwin's survival of the fittest.

The Nonconfrontationalists

The polar opposite of Steve the Gladiator is Jane, whose modus operandi is capitulation at all costs. Jane heads a social services agency, where she never, ever makes waves. Instead, she pushes everyone in her group to agree to a solution that satisfies no one. They settle for the lowest common denominator in order to avoid conflict.

Jane, a *Placater,* never puts herself in a direct line of fire. Whenever a meeting takes place, the participants roll their eyes and wait for Jane to restate someone else's point of view. Hiding from confrontation is Jane's primary mission, one that she performs very well, to the detriment of her department. Since they don't engage in the tough issues, they don't make real progress.

There are two other nonconfrontational types:

The Pollyanna. This person ignores tough issues. Pollyannas hope that problems or concerns will disappear without their involvement.

The Whiner. This type is known for being so unpleasant to other people that they concede the Whiner's point just to stop the nuisance. The Whiner's passive-aggressive behavior is especially aggravating.

While they're not in-your-face fighters, nonconfrontationalists still cause problems to fester and prevent positive action. By avoiding issues and making their coworkers' lives miserable, they create an unpleasant and unproductive environment for everyone.

HOPES STIMULATE GREAT RESULTS

If the fearmongers and consequences of the damaging cycle of fear and scarcity sound all too familiar, it's time to make a change. Fortunately, no matter how bad things look, it's possible to do. All people—yes, even the fighters and the nonconfrontationalists!—possess a positive spirit. That spirit may be shrouded in fear and thus difficult to find at the moment, but it can reveal itself in even the darkest and most contentious situations.

Tapping into this wellspring of spirit is the key to breaking the cycle of fear and getting results. The antidote to fear is hope.

People feel encouraged to explore their hopes when they suspend disbelief and entertain the idea that there is potential for improvement. And when they perceive common ground, they become more willing to participate in a cooperative process that

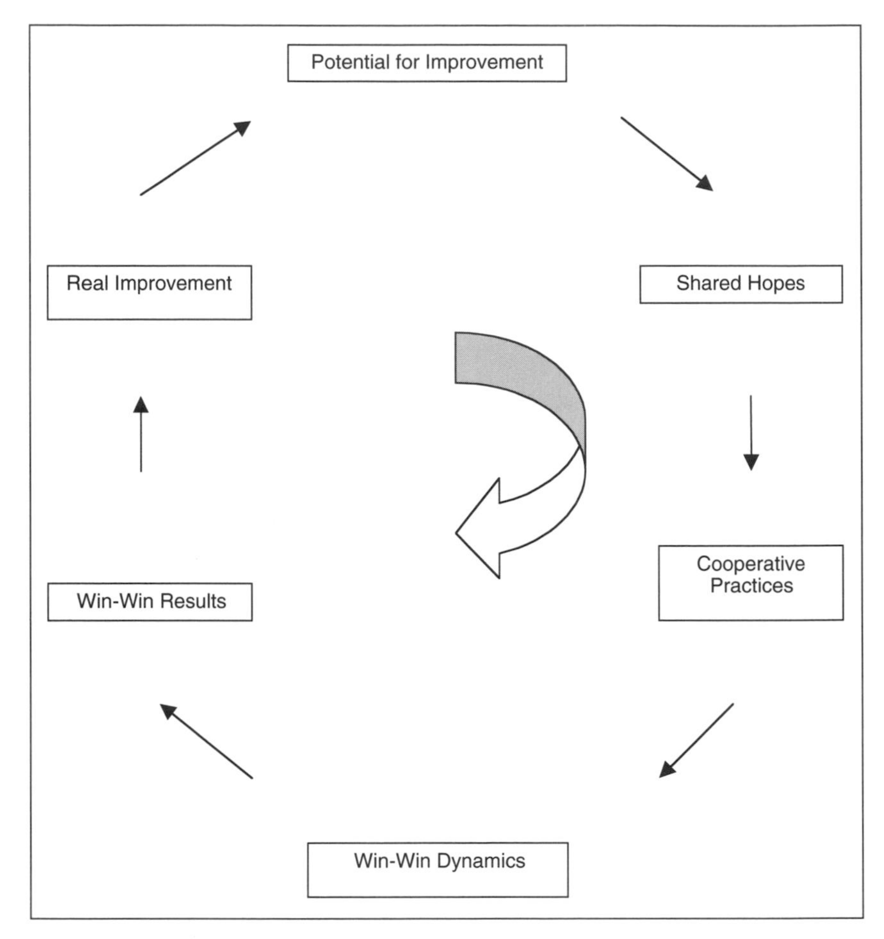

FIGURE 2 The cycle of hope and improvement.

stimulates win-win dynamics, which in turn produce win-win results (i.e., solutions that support the participants' shared hopes). The outcome is real improvement that encourages participants to sustain the cycle together. (See Figure 2.)

You don't have to believe that your situation will improve, however, in order to get started. Simply following the ten steps that guide you to explore your shared hopes and provide cooperative practices to realize them will get you going.

- Hopes draw on the aspirations and interests of everyone involved in the decision-making process.
- Hopes incorporate the deepest yearnings and accommodate diverse contributions.
- Hopes motivate.

Pursuing shared hopes, rather than fearful expectations, frees participants to identify and develop superior solutions. Considering the greater good (for oneself and the larger organization) is a radical concept in our individualistic culture. Yet it is exactly our willingness to let go of our own piece of the pie that is the first step in creating a more satisfying pie for all.

Hopes Boost Your Business

As used in this book, hopes are much more than positive thinking. They are the deepest aspirations participants have for their future. Hopes define what's most important to people about their organization and the issue at hand. As such, they energize and guide participants to thoughtful and successful results.

Hopes also serve as powerful magnets to attract customers, resources, and support. People respond enthusiastically to opportunities that fulfill their hopes.

For example, when I was the vice president of marketing for a start-up called Trade*Plus, which later became E*Trade, our goal was to give individual investors access to securities markets that only big institutional investors and brokers had. One customer, reflecting the wants of many, said, "I want technology to put me on the floor of the exchanges. I want to see the prices the brokers see. I want to put my orders in when I want, and I'd like to have all of the results organized and at my fingertips."

The company responded, developing technologies to fulfill these investors' hopes. Soon, our customers had a full suite of services with price quotes directly off the exchanges. They had the tools to place orders themselves, at any time of the day or night.

People flocked to the business. They weren't all small players, either. Some brought multi-million-dollar portfolios from full-service brokers. Investors who didn't wish to work with brokers—because of costs, language or communication difficulties, and many other reasons—reveled in their newfound freedom and power.

Our customers told us their hopes, and the company responded. Today E*Trade responds to the hopes of more than three million account holders. Hopes provided a powerful way to focus resources and stimulate great results.

THE PRACTICAL TEN-STEP PROCESS IS THE KEY TO POSITIVE CHANGE

We've established that hopes set the stage for positive change. The process of translating hopes into action is the instrument for realizing improvement in your decision making. The ten easy steps in this book are all you need to turn your hopes into reality. It doesn't matter how many people are seated around the table or how many different personal styles they bring with them—even deeply divided groups find they have common objectives or aspirations. What drives a wedge between people is not knowing the route to take in order to pursue their objectives.

Remember Tim and his R&D group? They found themselves in just this kind of situation. They needed to create an integrated set of tools to incorporate into millions of computers, but the different team members favored different approaches. Each knew what he or she personally desired and just wanted to push the other members to adopt it. Some even lacked the patience to listen to anyone with a different style or perspective.

When Tim and I introduced the ten-step process to the group, some of the people resisted the idea. Nevertheless, since prior attempts had failed to get them anywhere, the group members agreed to try the new approach.

When I asked the group to express their hopes for their work, we started to get somewhere. "I hope our work will be part of a product that makes computers much easier and friendlier for people to use," offered one researcher. "I hope we can build upon one another's work to create an integrated solution," suggested another. The remaining participants quickly followed in the same spirit: "I hope to enjoy working with my teammates." "I hope we attract more outstanding people, resources, and support to get the job done." "I hope we become known as an outstanding group of people who came together and made something special happen."

HOPES WORK

When hopes are part of the decision-making process, you have a whole new way of thinking and acting. Hopes stimulate

Positive thoughts: You hear statements like "We can do this together" and "I don't know what the solution is, but it's likely that something will fulfill what we want."

Upbeat feelings: Energy, confidence, and esprit de corps rise.

Affirmative behaviors: People become willing to listen, have more patience, and are alert to new ideas and opportunities.

Constructive relationships: Participants develop a cooperative attitude coupled with concern about solutions that will serve everyone involved.

As those seemingly contentious group members began to explore their hopes and why they were important to them, the tone and character of their interactions changed. They discovered that, despite all their bickering and dissension, they shared similar aspirations.

In the course of this pivotal meeting, the participants sorted through all of the issues and options and agreed upon the most desirable software for the team as a whole. They also identified an acceptable alternative in case they needed to make changes down the road.

But that's not all that happened. In addition to reaching two important decisions, they discovered that they could work together. This realization began a process of rebuilding trust, confidence, and mutual commitment. As a result, they gained something much more valuable than anything an open checkbook could buy. They found the human software to bring good people with a common purpose together to achieve great results in their business.

A Learning Process That Works—Human Software for Results

Many organizations think that decision making is a linear process. For them, it's all about assessing the situation, making a choice, and moving on.

In reality, effective decision making is a process of learning, which is more like a growth cycle. (See Figure 3.) Similar to computer software that provides a way to process information and reach conclusions, a group's decision procedure is the human software through which people process information and reach conclusions together. Effective decision making is actually effective learning.

Organizational success is a function of how quickly and effectively a group can move through the entire cycle and continue growing. Thus, making a quick decision that lacks the involvement and

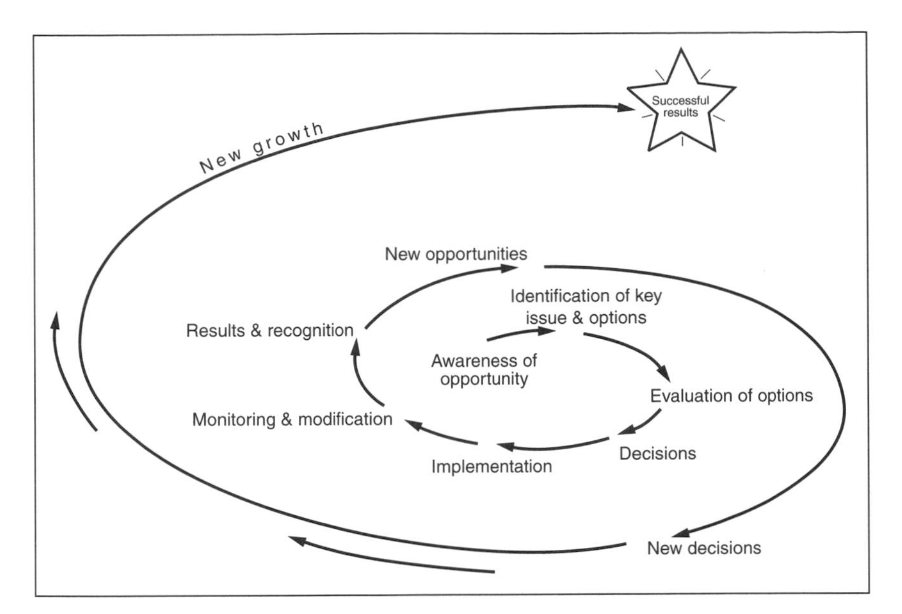

FIGURE 3 The decision process that encourages learning and gets results.

needed support of key stakeholders won't be successful. In fact, it often moves the process backward: People who have been left out must be brought up to speed on what's happening, which options were considered, and why the decision was made. Consequently, the organization loses momentum.

No matter what kind of group you're involved with or the types of people within it, thc dynamics of how that group makes decisions can change for the better. The ten-step process for decision making enables every group to

- Identify what is truly important to each person present
- Tap into each person's creative spirit and give everyone the opportunity to express this
- Find common ground to build on
- Multiply prospects for successful results

- Provide criteria for evaluating those results
- Give all involved something to celebrate

This process demonstrates an important truth: When you change a few things about the way people discuss and deal with issues, you can dramatically improve their degree of participation in any group effort and the results they achieve. You don't have to change who they are or what they think. This decision-making process simply invites participants to be their better selves and discover opportunities to work together that their fears and unproductive dynamics had previously hidden.

WHEN TO USE THIS PROCESS

The ten steps detailed in this book have been the foundation for breakthroughs in businesses that range from Fortune 500 companies to start-ups, and the growing firms in between. They've also worked for nonprofit organizations, government agencies, and different-size communities. (See Table 1.)

When should you put the ten steps to use? Whenever a situation arises in which group members need to make a decision and work together. You can also use the process to aid discussions and other business interactions. You can apply the process to decision-making situations in your community groups, in your relationships, and in everything you do. Practicing the process in one area will help you learn from it and use that learning to benefit other areas.

Another big plus of the ten-step process is that you can use it to "fix the rocket while it's in flight." That is, you can practice the process while you decide critical issues. Applying the process to the most important issues people face focuses their attention. It helps them realize that something important is at stake—whether it's how to design a new product or the critical priorities to set for their com-

TABLE 1 A Sample of Successful Applications of the Process

FORTUNE 500 COMPANIES
* Deciding on next generation of products
* Solving a multi-million-dollar production problem
* Improving industrial operations and maintenance
GROWTH BUSINESSES
* Dramatically boosting profits
* Expanding a specialty retail chain
* Resolving key roles in professional firm
GOVERNMENTS
* Gaining agreement on a contested new school
* Determining multi-million-dollar budget cuts
* Implementing computerized maintenance system
COMMUNITY AND NONPROFITS
* Agreeing on regional conservation
* Choosing a strategic direction
* Converting a budget deficit to a surplus

munity. When they discover that exciting outcomes are possible, they have a powerful motivation to overcome their fear-filled expectations and apply the process to other significant issues. They learn that success breeds success.

HOW LONG WILL IT TAKE?

Fears don't die easily. But progress can occur rapidly. It can take as little as thirty minutes of focused effort to see results (check out the 30-Minute Miracle technique in Strategy #1 to see how it's done), or the process may extend over several months, for example, if you're working with volunteers who gather information in their spare time and hold community meetings only once a month. The actual length of time will depend on the number of people involved and their diversity of interests. But even large, contentious groups can move ahead quickly. As groups become clear about their hopes, their decisions start to flow.

PUTTING THE PROCESS INTO PLAY

If you've been dreading facing your group because your problem-solving approach creates more problems than it solves, the solution you seek is at hand. Group decision making no longer needs to leave you exhausted, frustrated, and without hope. By putting the ten-step process to work, you can turn solving tough issues together into a positive, energizing experience. Just keep reading to learn how to

1. Enlist everyone
2. Discover your shared hopes
3. Uncover the real issues
4. Identify all options
5. Gather the right information
6. Get everything on the table
7. Write down choices that support your shared hopes
8. Map solutions
9. Look ahead
10. Stay charged up

And make great decisions.

The Quick Use Guide is a good way to track the steps as you read about them. (See Table 2.)

TABLE 2 Quick Use Guide: Ten Easy Steps for Reaching Agreement

STEP	BRIEF DESCRIPTION
Step #1: **Enlist everyone**	Whom can we involve who knows something about this issue or will need to participate in a decision about it or in its implementation? Each person is important to get real results.
Step #2: **Discover shared hopes**	Before we get started or anyone jumps to specific solutions, let's spend a few minutes to hear what each person hopes will result from the effort and why that's important.
Step #3: **Uncover the real issues**	I'm not sure that the issue is really clear. It might be exactly as you've said, but let's explore it a little further. How about if we each take a few moments to express our thoughts and concerns about the topic? Before the next person speaks, let's have that person paraphrase what the previous speaker said so that we know that we've really heard it clearly.
Step #4: **Identify all options**	It's good brainstorming to get lots of options out on the table before we discuss any one in detail. We can go around the group and have each person offer an option that might help fulfill what we hope to accomplish. Let's not repeat anything or start agreeing or disagreeing.
Step #5: **Gather the right information**	Rather than gather information about each option on its own, we can organize our efforts by our hopes and look at all of the options from the perspective of what we really want to accomplish. That way, we will work together and efficiently collect the information we need.
Step #6: **Get everything on the table**	We could save a lot of time and debate if we went around the group and had everyone state something that might be negative about each option and did the same with the potential positives. I'm sure that we could each find something to say both pro and con about each option without repeating one another. It won't take much time to hear everyone's perspectives, and we'll avoid divisive debates. We're also likely to think of even better options.

TABLE 2 *Continued*

STEP	BRIEF DESCRIPTION
Step #7: **Write down choices that support shared hopes**	Let's find out what each person candidly thinks about the choices. Each person can list what looks best to fulfill our hopes and any acceptable alternatives. This straw ballot will give us a snapshot of possible solutions.
Step #8: **Map solutions**	We can tabulate the results on a flip chart or piece of paper to sort out all of the options. Then, we can look at possible ways to improve upon the most attractive alternatives and find a solution that everyone will support.
Step #9: **Look ahead**	Before we rush off to implement our solution, we need a backup plan and early opportunities to see how our solution performs and compares with acceptable alternatives.
Step #10: **Stay charged up**	People did a great job of listening to one another and searching for solutions that will serve the best interests of the group. Let's bring everyone together and hear from people about how the results support the hopes we share. It's time to celebrate what we've accomplished and encourage people to continue working together effectively.

BE AN AGENT OF HOPE

Be aware of your own cycles of fear and hope. Write down for yourself what your thoughts, feelings, behaviors, and relationships with others are like in each cycle. These are your cues to determine which frame of mind you've chosen. If you find yourself in the fearful mode, do some self-examination to determine whether you truly are in imminent danger or can choose to be your hopeful self. Your choice will make a big difference for you and the people with whom you work.

PART 2

Ten Easy Steps for Reaching Agreement

HOW TO USE EACH STEP AND GAIN PRACTICAL VALUE

Part 2 explains how to do each step. You'll see why every step is important and how the steps link together. Examples demonstrate the bottom-line value of using them to translate your hopes into concrete results.

Each step is its own chapter and includes the following elements:

- **Step #___in Action**
  Read about tough issues in business, government, and community organizations that this step has solved. See how the use of this step contributed to a great decision.
- **The Keys to Step #___**
  Learn why this step is valuable. Discover the dynamics and nuances of using it effectively.
- **Putting Step #___into Practice**
  Follow a clear checklist that aids you in applying this step to your own tough issue. Find tools you can use to jump-start your efforts.

As you read about each step, think about opportunities to apply it in your work. Embrace the opportunity to make a difference and enjoy a positive and productive decision-making process. Jot down any concerns you have about using the steps. Part 3 will give you strategies to overcome obstacles.

STEP #1

Enlist Everyone

Invite Hidden as Well as Visible Talent and Avoid Creating Enemies

Inspiration is everywhere.
—Anonymous

Tough issues aren't just the venue of executives and managers. They affect everyone in the group or organization, from the most senior management people to the newest hire, from the captain of the police force to the newest family in the community. Where companies and organizations are concerned, every person in the group must be counted on to give his or her opinions and share experiences.

But, too often, that doesn't happen. Instead, a counterproductive mind-set prevails, one defined by negativity and all-too-familiar statements like these:

- "There's not enough time to involve everyone."
- "Some people can't be trusted. They have their own agendas that might disrupt our plans."
- "It's just not possible to manage input from everyone."

When those kinds of fears run rampant, it's just a small step to a limited and unproductive conclusion:

"Let's just get a small group together and work something out." There is a better, inclusive approach, and you need to put it into practice right at the start.

STEP #1 IN ACTION

Tough Issue: *Computer System Can't Get off the Ground*

Greg, the manager of a municipal water system, faced a big problem. His team needed to implement a computerized preventive maintenance system. For several years, the water division had tried to put a computerized system into operation, but the project went nowhere. Management wanted the system, but the union workers resisted it.

The workers had lots of reasons for avoiding the change. "We don't have time to learn a new system and do our jobs at the same time," some said. "Not everyone would have access to the equipment," others complained. "We haven't decided how to switch from our manual system to an automated maintenance scheduling and tracking program," still others grumbled.

Their points of view came from fear and worry about scarcity. Learn a new skill? Maybe that meant their old jobs, which they knew so well, were going to be phased out. Not have access to equipment? That might mean there would not be enough to go around. Not make the decision to switch? That was fear-based procrastination, pure and simple.

But they had to implement the system. The aging water system needed planned maintenance and it had become too complex to track efficiently with manual methods. With all the worries and fears, though, how could the managers and dozens of frontline workers come to terms and steer the water system into the future?

A Great Decision Solution

The situation in which Greg and the rest of the water division found themselves seemed hopeless. Greg knew he had to move the project ahead, but it looked too mired down for any optimism.

Greg started with the traditional management approach of selecting a group of six people to resolve the dilemma. This small group consisted of managers and workers as well as computer specialists—the obvious stakeholders and people you might expect would have the answers.

However, the solution to the real problem—getting worker buy-in—didn't come from the traditional work group approach. It came from employing the full power of Step #1—inviting all of the talent at hand, whether it was front and center or on the sidelines, to solve the problem. Here's how they did it.

Greg brought the problem to all fifty members of the utilities department workforce. He invited anyone from the department with relevant ideas or experience to join the task force.

This reaped great results. The most valuable contribution came from the most unexpected source—a maintenance worker in the separate sewer division. Tom, a blue-collar union member, had experience with the implementation of a computerized maintenance system at a former job. Because he had been invited, he offered to share his know-how. "I know how you can do this," Tom offered. "We put in a system like this at my previous job. I was skeptical at first, and it took some adjustments. Once we got it going, however, it made everyone's job better."

The rank and file of the water division valued the expertise of a fellow worker and consequently lent their support to the plan for the new system. It was a defining moment. By moving beyond the traditional limited group approach and instead including everyone, the project went ahead, backed with enthusiasm, and produced solid results.

Tough Issue: *$250 Million Project Hits Wall of Resistance*

A Fortune 500 corporation wanted to add a $250 million production facility on the property of its existing plant. It developed detailed plans on its own and announced them to the local community. Since no one in the community had known about the plans, much less had the *opportunity to discuss them, the project met stiff resistance. "I just about fell out of my chair when I heard about it," said the mayor. Even people sympathetic to the company's presence in the community felt blindsided.*

Fearing that they would never have a voice in the planning, city officials launched a full-scale legal effort to block the project. The company's detailed plan, which it had spent a million dollars to develop, crashed and burned. But the company needed the facility. What could it do next?

A Great Decision Solution

What the company managers did was to shift gears and invite everyone in the city government and in local community groups to share their interests and develop a plan together. The outcome was a win-win solution. The corporation obtained support from the city to double the capacity of its new production facility compared to the original plan. In turn, the company committed to removing the old plant, creating bike paths, freeing up unneeded land for new community uses, and providing a reliable stream of revenue to the city for its other needs.

THE KEYS TO STEP #1

Put Faith in the Stakeholders

Rigid, limited viewpoints prevent groups from considering crucial information. For example, a product development group rushing to meet a deadline might skip testing its product with typical customers. Senior management might launch a new service initiative without involving the people who will execute it.

In sharp contrast to this opaque thinking, casting a broad, open net improves the breadth and quality of ideas, which often come from

Step #1 works wonders for community organizations, too. For example, in one community of 10,000, the 25-person police force was pushed to the limits. Crime grew along with the population, but the budget for the force did not. Somehow, the police had to figure out a way to get greater control over a population 400 times the size of the department.

But many fears blocked progress. The civilian population felt that the police didn't have time for their concerns. Their fear was that their complaints would be overlooked, that their families and businesses wouldn't get the protection they needed and deserved, and that crime would escalate. For their part, the stressed-out police worried that they couldn't control the increasing problems they faced. How could they deal with the rising tide of security problems and the public's expectations for safety?

What they did was reach out. The police chief invited service clubs, citizens' organizations, and neighborhood interest groups to discuss public safety. From this dialogue, many ideas emerged on how the community could help the police. In addition to neighborhood watch programs, community service volunteers became an active part of police activities. Through the creative ideas and energy from the broad range of participants, the community joined with the police to reach every neighborhood while remaining within the department's budget. The innovative solutions not only improved public safety but also strengthened links across the community and among its neighborhoods.

people who are not traditional decision makers. By including everyone and tapping into their expanse of experience, you will achieve something even more important: You will avoid creating enemies.

Enemies Are Made, Not Hired

When people feel left out of the decision-making process, it causes more than bruised egos. Leaving people out erodes trust and confidence. It also costs time and opportunity because the people making the decision need more time to find a solution or they miss important ideas when they're not working with all possible contributors. They also need extra time to explain the ultimate decision to those whom they left out. People who have been left out will want to know about the issues and options that were considered and how participants reached the conclusion they did. Excluding people from the process overturns the funnel of information and makes a mess. (See Figure 4.)

When those who have been left out express their dissension, as they almost inevitably do, the group can't move forward. Instead, it splits apart. Any goodwill that existed is destroyed because those who were excluded now believe that their ideas will never get a fair hearing. "They've already made up their minds; why should I even try to tell them what I think?" is the reasoning of the ignored.

Whether the exclusion is intentional or unintentional, the

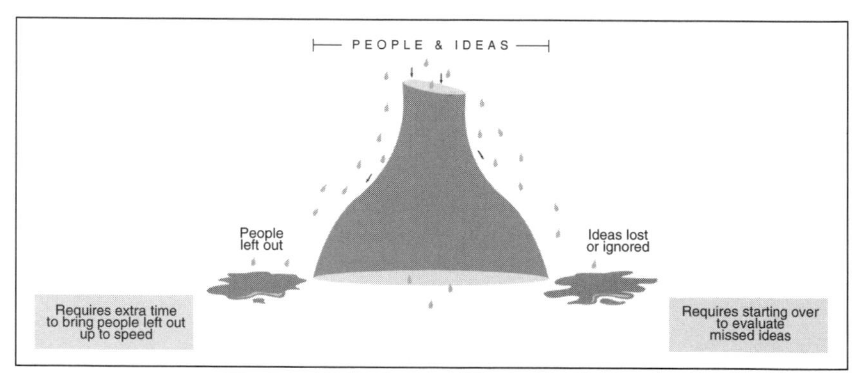

FIGURE 4 Excluding people wastes time and misses opportunities.

small-minded action undermines one of the most powerful learning experiences for group members. Leaving people out precludes the opportunity for groups to air their ideas, change their minds, or accept something new without losing face. Exclusionary tactics push people further into the field of fear.

Funnel People and Ideas into the Process

It doesn't have to be that way. By enlisting everyone, you can garner the best ideas and encourage cooperative effort. Turn the funnel right side up, and draw people and ideas into your working group to make great decisions together. (See Figure 5.)

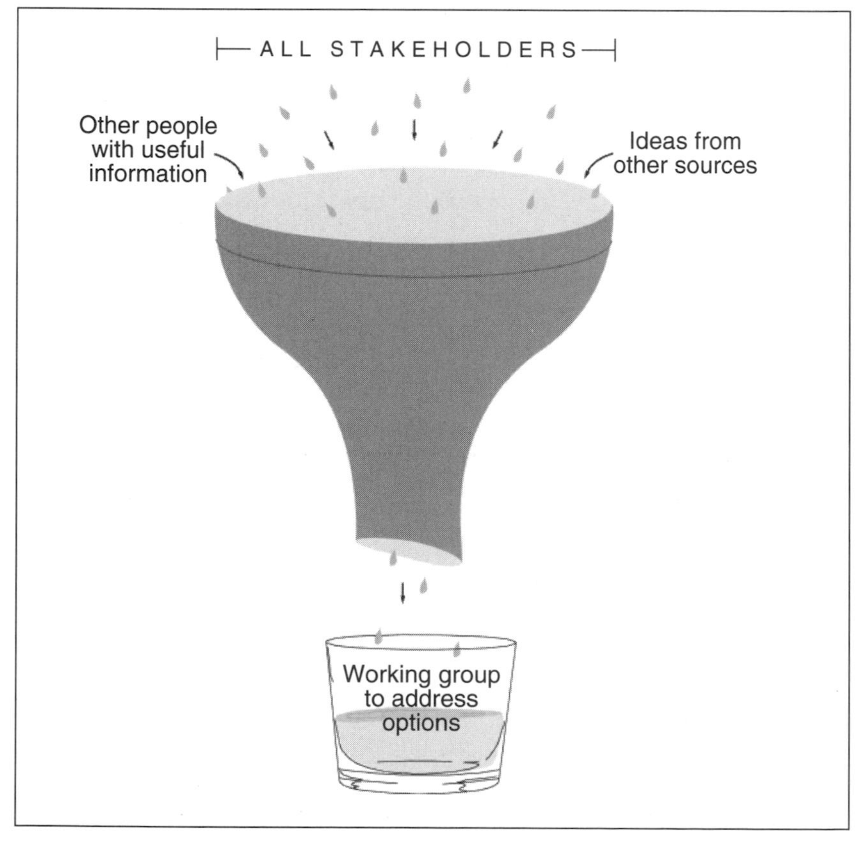

FIGURE 5 Funnel everyone and their ideas and you get better results.

Build Shared Ownership

Focus on how you can encourage all persons with a stake or useful information to participate in the process. More than involvement, you want shared ownership for the discussions and their success.

For example, when the corporate leaders of the $250 million project shifted to an inclusive approach, they asked representatives from local business and community groups for advice on how to reach out. Who needed to be involved? When and where would it be best to meet? How can we promote a constructive dialogue? The informal representatives guided the company to constructive participants and the best arrangements to attract their involvement. Further, the representatives agreed to distribute notices and personally encourage attendance.

This shift to shared ownership for the meetings brought critically important government decision makers and even skeptical constituencies into the discussions. The dynamic shifted from the corporation pushing its project against fierce resistance to a mode of "let's look at the issues and opportunities together." Step #1 created the conditions for a positive process to begin.

Include Group Members Who Can't Attend a Meeting

There's no excuse to leave out people who aren't physically available. For one thing, you can get in touch with them before a meeting and ask for their input, including comments related to the next steps in the ten-step process. When you talk, ask them the following questions:

- What they hope will be accomplished
- What their thoughts, feelings, and perspectives are on the issues that the group needs to address
- If they have any possible solutions they would like to have considered

- What negatives or positives they want to share about those options

Another approach is to ask attendees to represent the missing people and voice what they believe their input might be. (Frequently, all the people involved know each other's perspectives well.) In the discussions about the new production facility, the team even added a chair for each missing party and wrote the organization's or person's name on it. This gave the entire group a physical reminder of important interests and the need to consider their perspectives. No one was "out of sight, out of mind."

Count on Everyone: The Sum Is Greater Than the Parts

Involving more people than just the key players also improves dynamics within a group. The additional players become leavening agents, who shift relationships and stimulate new perspectives. As a result, people work together better, progress accelerates, and results rise to new heights.

The inclusive approach contrasts with typical approaches that focus only on the primary protagonists. For example, some exclusive approaches send deeply divided parties off to work out their differences. That's like tossing flour, water, and yeast into a pressure cooker and hoping that the dough will rise. It intensifies fear-filled dynamics and undermines the goodwill needed for successful and sustained results.

Still other ineffective approaches use time-consuming and costly "shuttle diplomacy" between warring factions. In those situations, the person playing diplomat bears the burden of producing results, and the principals don't hear and learn from one another directly. This approach is like trying to bake bread without mixing the ingredients. Although it avoids direct conflict, it doesn't yield rich results.

In contrast, inclusion works as the first step in getting great results because it leads to the remaining steps, which provide ways for even deeply divided people to work together constructively. Focusing on 100 percent sharing of information reduces divisive debate to zero and brings out participants' best ideas. Including all of the people who are going to be affected by a decision—and others who have valuable ideas—enhances trust, builds confidence, and prevents the power plays that undermine the potential for cooperative action.

PUTTING STEP #1 INTO PRACTICE

1. *Include everyone the decision will affect.* This means you need to identify the interests of each person and each group having a stake in the outcome. If you have a question about whether or not to involve someone, err on the side of inclusion. Remember to keep the funnel wide at the start. It's far better to let people drop out of the process if they discover that they won't be affected by the result than to make them into enemies by excluding them in the beginning.

2. *Invite anyone who may have useful information.* Make a list of those people who have had a similar experience or have knowledge about the issues at hand. Between phone, fax, and e-mail, you can gather data on a virtual basis.

3. *Cast your net wider.* Invite others to share their insights and perspectives. Some of the best input often comes from unexpected sources. Reassure all participants that you will respect their views.

4. *Make sure that those who should be present at a meeting are there.* Get key interests involved in identifying participants and making arrangements for the meetings. Build ownership in the process. Sometimes people may be skeptical or reluctant to play a part in the solution process. Talk to them and tell them that

their opinions are important and highly regarded. Invite their input—and mean it.

5. *Use the Inclusion Checklist.* This simple chart will help you enlist everyone who needs to be part of the decision process. (See Figure 6.)

Inclusion Checklist.			
Participants	**Invited**	**Participating**	**Other forms of input**
Who needs to make the final decision?			
Who needs to implement it?			
Whom will the decision affect?			
Who may have useful information or ideas?			
Who else might we ask for helpful perspectives?			

FIGURE 6 Inclusion Checklist.

BE AN AGENT OF HOPE

Inclusiveness is one of the first casualties of fear. Include everyone who has a stake in the topic, and reach out to others who may have useful information. The steps and strategies that follow will provide ways to involve them constructively and efficiently.

STEP #2

Discover Shared Hopes

Multiply Your Prospects for Success

We must rediscover the distinction
between hope and expectation.
—Ivan Illich

Many groups are hope-less. They don't lack potential, but they do lack clarity about what's truly important to them. This deficiency blocks group members from engaging with one another, discovering effective solutions, and working together effectively.

You can turn around any troubling group situation by asking participants two questions:

1. What are your hopes?
2. Why are they important to you?

These disarmingly simple questions initiate discussion about what's really important and why. They invite participants to look deeply into themselves and share their findings with one another.

STEP #2 IN ACTION

Tough Issue: *Owner's Expectations Stifle Business*

Ted's unreasonable expectations stifled his business and endangered his health. As an owner of a growing, profitable enterprise, he thought, "I ought to be in charge of the biggest division." So he tried to juggle dozens of employees and the rising demands of sophisticated client projects. But the job was effectively eating him up—he popped antacids all day long. His role didn't fit him. Although the business had great potential, Ted's fixed concept of his role both held the business back and diminished his enjoyment.

A Great Decision Solution

Ted's expectation was that he *ought* to manage the largest unit in the company. At an emotional level, however, the job tied his stomach in knots.

When asked what his deepest hopes were, Ted responded that he hoped to build a profitable business, expand opportunities for his employees, and gain more free time with his family. He realized that his expectations held him back from fulfilling these aspirations. When he asked his employees what their hopes were, he discovered they were similar.

Freed from what he thought he *should* do, Ted worked with his team to designate someone else to lead the largest unit—an option he had not imagined at the outset. Within five years, the business more than tripled in revenues, and profits expanded even faster. What's more important, Ted stopped popping antacids. "I like my role and I like the business more than ever," he beamed. Now both he and his employees enjoy a healthy, profitable enterprise.

Tough Issue: *Demanding Objectives Need Broad Support*

Rick, the general manager of a $300 million technology business, had less than six weeks to turn around results and meet the parent company's *profit target for the year. "I've got some ideas about what needs to be done and I'm committed, but I'm not sure my top managers are," he said. "We don't have much time, and I'm going to be drawn away on a special project for most of the little time we have. And our offsite planning session is later this week." He worried about how he could get everybody on board and the turnaround under way.*

A Great Decision Solution

A typical manager in Rick's shoes might have ignored the potential disconnect with his team and plowed forward. Others would have emphasized the corporate goals and tried to rally the team around them, subtly referring to the wrath of the parent company if they didn't make their numbers—a fear-driven approach. Sure, Rick could have played cheerleader or cajoler, but then his managers would have been running off of his energy rather than contributing their own. Rick wanted to find a better path.

He began by thinking about how to engage his key managers and realize the objectives of their $300 million business. He followed the advice from Step #2: He asked all of his team members to write down their hopes for the business in order to find out what was really important to them and why. He encouraged them to tap into their own aspirations and motivation.

The results exceeded his expectations. He reported, "We not only found a few 'silver bullets' to make this year's numbers, but also discovered an idea that may be an industry-changing 'platinum bullet' that will help us soar." By asking all team members to reach deep inside themselves and discover what they truly hoped for, Rick unleashed his team's internal energy, and everyone enjoyed the results.

But it's not enough just to write down your hopes and why they are important to you. There's a special energy that comes alive in dialogue with another person. Even if you are dealing with an issue on your own, have someone listen to your hopes and ask why they are important to you. You'll discover new insights and opportunities.

THE KEYS TO STEP #2

Use Hopes to Break Through Limiting Expectations

Successful businesspeople and civic leaders create breakthrough opportunities because they don't limit themselves with preconceptions. One of the best ways to find relief for struggling people or organizations is to examine their expectations. Often, people's pain lies in some attachment to a fixed outcome. They feel stuck in a certain role or path. Conflicts within organizations or communities usually arise from clashes between differing sets of expectations.

Hopes will free participants from limiting preconceptions. Remember Ted, the business owner? His expectation that he should run the biggest division in the company resulted in an emotional nightmare and stifled growth. But once he divested himself of his preconception and tuned in to his hopes, he could expand his business and happily reach his goals.

Use Hopes to Unify Diverse Interests

In more than ten years of facilitating dozens of groups—including combative managers, litigants, and political opposites—I've yet to find a situation in which participants couldn't agree upon a shared set of hopes. A particularly difficult situation involved a spirited community group that battled in court for the right to hold a Mardi Gras parade. The city officials and local business owners worried that the event had become uncontrollable and posed a danger to participants and bystanders. "Someone's going to get killed," they feared. After the different sides spent hundreds of hours and thousands of dollars on legal fees, the judge ruled that the group had a right to hold the parade. He directed the parties to work out a plan that fairly divided the responsibilities.

Although the court case granted the right to parade, it didn't determine how the different interests would work together. Both sides wondered how they could agree on a plan when the bitter lawsuit had left so much anger and distrust.

Following Step #2, both parties explored what was really important to each person involved and worked to understand why. Every person wrote down his or her hopes on sheets of paper. Then each participant found the person whom he or she knew least well and asked that person Step #2's important questions: "What is your hope?" and "Why is it important to you?" The room of forty people buzzed with conversation.

As divergent as their interests had been, all participants appreciated and supported the hopes they heard. The police discovered that the parade organizers shared their concern about safety. Similarly, both police and city officials acknowledged the importance to community members of a creative outlet. In less than an hour's time, all participants discovered that they shared common hopes. With this encouraging foundation, they worked together to develop an effective plan.

The targeted time spent discussing hopes within a business or organization generates much more value than the often-lengthy discussions of "mission" and "vision." Mission and vision statements represent a struggle to distill diversity into pithy phrases, which too often squeeze the life out of what people felt when they created them. On the other hand, hopes capture employees' and participants' deep yearnings and accommodate the multiple interests inherent in today's communities and workplaces.

Use Hopes to Uncover Solutions Where None Existed

Hopes are important in getting people to work together, but they play an even more powerful role in expanding and improving solutions. Each time you ask someone why a particular hope is important to him or her, you'll multiply the prospects for a successful outcome—often tenfold or more!

For example, Rosa, a college professor, desired a more diverse faculty and staff at the college where she taught. "I want the people who work here to be more representative of the overall student body," she said. Since few faculty and staff left their positions, however, opportunities to hire more diverse colleagues rarely occurred. Other faculty members heard Rosa's concerns, but felt there was little they could do about it because of the current hiring freeze and formal hiring practices. Making progress toward Rosa's goal seemed unlikely.

Rosa's first expression of her hope for a more diverse faculty and staff was at the surface level and had no practical solution. There was little that she could do, and, short of retiring early to make way for replacements, her colleagues couldn't do much to help, either. But when Rosa really considered why diversity was important to her, she went to a deeper level. She realized that she'd like the students to have role models for success in their own careers. She went still deeper and realized that she wanted students to know that, regardless of their circumstances, they could make it in the world. This deeper aspiration stimulated ideas for immediate solutions. Successful women business owners, professionals of different ethnicities, and various other types of resource people could visit the campus as guest lecturers and invite students to serve as interns with them. Service clubs and outside speakers could profile opportunities and mentor students. Curricula could incorporate case studies highlighting diverse racial and ethnic interests. Counselors, community members, and others could rally behind the objective.

Simply asking "Why?" allowed Rosa to punch through the surface issue and tap into her underlying hope. Dozens of opportunities and ways in which others could support her objective resulted. The process of exploring Rosa's original hope was like digging a well: It was necessary that she plumb for each underlying hope until she reached the deep aquifer of interests and resources that others could share and act upon. (See Figure 7.)

Use Hopes to Avoid the "Devil in the Details"

Hopes help participants in decision-making groups realize that they share common objectives and can avoid needless frustration. Without expressing their hopes, many group members waste time bicker-

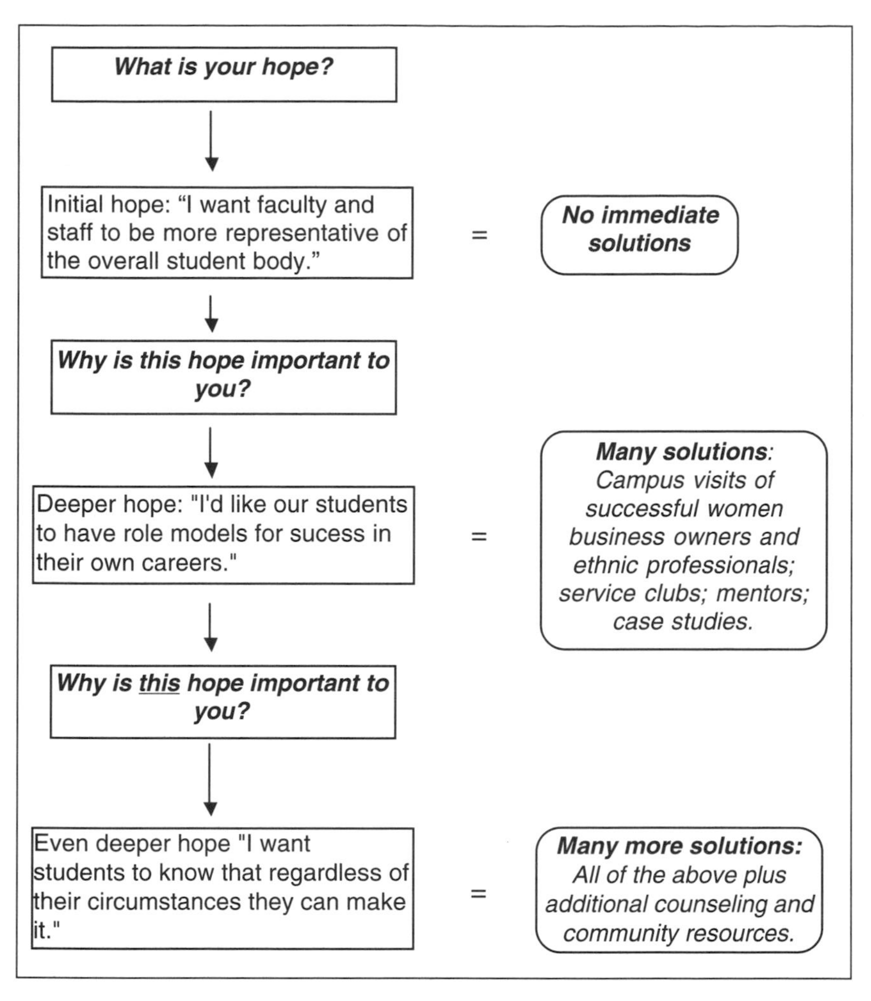

FIGURE 7 Plumbing the depths of Rosa's hopes.

ing with one another about small issues because they haven't discovered their shared direction. People fight for control of the steering wheel because they don't trust where others might take them if they relinquished it. Clarifying participants' underlying hopes and where they are headed in the big picture saves time in figuring out how to get there.

Unfortunately, businesses, government agencies, and community groups often plunge right into the details of an issue, even when they know that they'll be troublesome. They feel resigned to frustration and proceed to trudge through the pain. They also resist exploring their hopes. "We've got real work to do," they say. "There's no time to explore or share our hopes." Sadly, they deny themselves a proven path to great decision making and the successful solutions that result.

Betty, the mayor of a medium-size city, and the members of the city council are a good example. "The devil is in the details," Betty intoned as she started the city council's discussion of a controversial issue. As mayor, she wanted to be a strong leader who faces issues head-on and resolves them. She thought it was a sign of leadership—the right stuff of management—to wade into the details of key projects the city needed to prioritize.

It didn't take more than a few minutes, however, for the participants to start bickering over those details. After two hours of flexing their mental muscles with one another, the council remained embroiled in the details. There was much heat but little light, and goodwill diminished as participants argued their views. Resolution of the issue seemed remote.

Betty was right. The details were devilish. However, Betty had underestimated their power.

Betty and her fellow council members needn't have wallowed fruitlessly in the details of their civic project. Had they plumbed their hopes—asking What do we want to accomplish? Why is it important to our community? What are alternative ways to get there?—they would have been on the path to resolution.

Once they learned to put Step #2 into play, Betty and the city council had much more success. A particularly sticky issue concerned juvenile delinquency and violence. Mark, an action-oriented city council member, thought he had the solution. He arrived at a city council meeting with a fixed agenda in mind: He wanted the city to build a new park. He touted it as a critical project to reduce juvenile delinquency and urged expedited action. To bolster his case, Mark proposed an available site and presented letters of support for the park from teachers and parents concerned about the juvenile delinquency threat.

However, Martha, another council member and an ardent environmentalist committed to preserving open space, immediately condemned the plan. She didn't want precious open space at the edge of the city developed into a park that might stimulate more growth.

Chuck, the self-declared fiscal watchdog on the council, objected to the drain on city funds to build and maintain the park. He demanded to know just where the money would come from. He decried the park initiative as another unproven and fiscally irresponsible program.

Mark's plan triggered Martha's and Chuck's fears and it looked like the meeting would get mired down in divisive debate. Mark was reeling from the opposition to his idea. He felt angry and dejected that his idea didn't get a fair hearing.

Before the situation could get worse, Betty asked Mark about his hopes for the project—what he hoped to accomplish and why that was important to him. Mark explained his desire to reduce juvenile delinquency by providing more activities for local youth. This hope went deeper than the details that had pushed Martha's and Chuck's hot buttons. With the situation calmer and the intent more clear, the council members agreed on their underlying objective. Thus, they had a place to start.

The council members discussed ways to realize their shared hope, and new options emerged. For example, they proposed asking the local school district to open school gymnasiums after hours for recreational activities. This option satisfied Mark's objective for immediate action, and, as a bonus, they could put it into action more quickly than developing a new park. The option also satisfied Martha's desire to protect open space. And Chuck appreciated that it involved no new capital expenditures and only limited incremental operating expenses for supervision and extended janitorial services. Everyone agreed that if the program didn't work, the city could terminate it without a long-term commitment.

Attractive solutions like this one arise when groups start with their hopes and later examine the options and develop the details.

The more deeply a group plumbs its hopes, the greater the array of options it uncovers. For example, if the council members had continued to discuss why more activities to reduce juvenile delinquency were important, they might have highlighted the desire for the city's youth to develop a solid set of values and a shared sense of community. Then dozens of additional options, such as asking service clubs and social service agencies for their ideas and resources, could be employed to fulfill that hope.

Use your hopes to take the agony out of the details. By first exploring and confirming the hopes you share, participants in your group will be motivated to work together and to more easily resolve the issues you face.

Use Hopes to Improve and Sustain Results

An industrial facility with decades of conflict between its operations and maintenance departments found new strength when employees articulated their hopes. These rivals had bickered with one another like two old enemies trapped in endless strife. "Those guys in maintenance don't fix our equipment properly," complained an operations supervisor. "The equipment wouldn't break down so often," countered a maintenance worker, "if the operators followed procedures."

But when these warring camps met and explored their hopes, the participants discovered they shared similar aspirations, which included the following:

- To become a *team* [their emphasis]
- To work together to accomplish goals
- To have *everyone* [their emphasis] feel good about the work they do
- To be the benchmark plant, setting the standards for others to follow

They charted these and another twelve hopes and identified ways to realize them together. At the start, they figured that they were only about halfway toward fulfillment of their hopes. Six months later, both groups surveyed their members to assess their progress. "We've achieved over 70 percent of our long-term hopes," the maintenance manager reported. "With continued efforts together," the operations manager added, "our combined team is confident that we can realize over 90 percent of our shared hopes." They had overcome their seemingly intractable differences and found a new path to better results.

Connect with Your Deepest Hopes

In a culture often driven by fear and greed, connecting with our deepest hopes can be difficult. In fact, it may take you several responses to Step #2's important questions for you to discover your underlying hopes. Take your time. It's a worthwhile investment. If you have difficulties, these suggestions can help.

Look for the Flip Side of Your Greatest Fear

As you think about your hopes, plunge into the depths of your worst nightmare. What troubles you most? Left with our fears, catastrophe can loom before us. For example, you might worry that your customers won't be able to afford your products and you won't have the revenues to meet your expenses.

> *Hope is brightest when it dawns from fears.*
> —Sir Walter Scott

The way out of the quagmire is to look at the flip side of your fear to find your hope. For example, if you fear losing customers, your hope will be to offer distinctive solutions to their problems. Then, instead of worrying about the economic downturn, think about new opportunities to serve customers' needs. Shift your mindset from thinking of your product or service as a cost to becoming a source of new revenue for your customers.

Appreciate What You Have

There's a meditative exercise that asks you to carefully observe and then slowly eat a single raisin. It's amazing what tastes and textures you discover while doing this, instead of simply regarding the raisin as an insignificant and overly familiar dried-up grape, if you even think of it at all. When I eat my lunch with this kind of contemplative spirit, I'm satisfied with half the amount of food (which is good for my waistline!). My appetite is not fixed. I can influence it by appreciating what I have before me.

When you appreciate what you have, you also gain perspective on what you really need to do next, rather than what you feel driven to do. In a business situation, you don't chase after miscellaneous opportunities; you focus your attention on what fits with your business and will yield distinctive value to others. You thereby accomplish your goals more effectively and efficiently.

If you have less than you want in your business or community organization, take some time to appreciate what you already have. For example, the quickest way to get more customers is to appreciate the ones you have. Invite them to a dinner or a reception together. Let them know how important they are to you. Encourage them to share their stories with one another. They will help you find more customers.

Choose Hope, Not Fear

Several years ago, a fledgling rural church faced a huge budget shortfall, with projected revenues 20 percent below its basic expenses. Members of the church could have easily said, "This is a crisis. We have to find ways to retrench." Instead, the treasurer presented the issue to the church's board by saying, "We have an invitation to find creative ministries that excite people, make a meaningful difference in their lives, and also attract new resources."

The group went on to start an abundance shop (its distinctive version of a traditional thrift store), sell fresh Christmas trees, and offer programs and materials to help people deal with difficult issues of fear, anger, and rejection. As a result, the church balanced its budget with some to spare and attracted a significant number of new members.

PUTTING STEP #2 INTO PRACTICE

1. *Ask all participants to write down their hopes—their deepest aspirations—for the group.* After a few moments of reflection about what's important, use a bold marker and write one hope per sheet on 8½- by 11-inch paper. Use as many sheets of paper as you have hopes. Your hopes do not need to be currently attainable. Mark those that are most compelling to you with an asterisk.

2. *Pair up people who know each other least well and have them ask each other, "Why is your hope important to you?" The listener records what the partner says.* Hopes come alive in dialogue with others. Asking people why something is important to them often triggers deeper answers. Both people in a pair should be accurate reporters of what they hear. Don't distract the other person by agreeing or debating, trying to find solutions, or doing anything other than faithfully listening and writing down a summary of what the person says. The process builds goodwill. You'll be amazed at what you learn.

3. *Share the hopes with the full group. Identify common themes.* If you have a large group, post the hopes on the wall and ask several people to help cluster similar hopes together. Often, the hopes crystallize around several themes: relationships, resources, results, and rewards.

4. *Check whether each person supports the hopes of the other participants.* Even very divisive groups can agree upon a shared set of hopes. Since the hopes include everyone's perspectives and don't impose a single view, they invite support. One element reflects many perspectives—like the facets of a diamond.

5. *Use your hopes to focus your discussions.* If your group gathers for several meetings to discuss a topic, read the hopes at the start of each meeting. Have each person read a hope until you have completed the list. This will center the group on its broader purpose.

6. *Let go of your need to set outcomes so that your shared hopes can come alive.* Trust that something better can happen for your group than the result you may have expected.

7. *Use your list of shared hopes to evaluate opportunities and track your group's progress.* You'll see how to put your hopes into practice in Steps #3 through #10.

BE AN AGENT OF HOPE

The most powerful thing you can do to reach agreement on even the toughest issues is to help participants in your group discover their deepest hopes. Your shared hopes are waiting to come alive, if only you ask the right questions and listen to the responses.

STEP #3

Uncover the Real Issues

Listen to Thoughts and Feelings

Not knowing when the dawn will come,
I open every door.
—Emily Dickinson

One of the biggest pitfalls in solving tough issues is failing to identify the real issue. You can't solve a problem, especially a tough one, unless you know what the real issue is.

My experience with groups from start-ups to Fortune 500 companies to community organizations shows that groups misidentify the key issue more than 50 percent of the time. That doesn't mean that whatever they have before them isn't an issue, but it's not the issue that's preventing their agreement and successful results.

Focusing on the wrong issue will never solve the problem. What's worse, it frustrates participants and diminishes their willingness to work together. How many times have you "solved" a problem people presented to you and discovered that they weren't satisfied with your perfectly good solution? You addressed the issue they presented, but you didn't address the real issue, the one that was at the root of the problem.

To get to the real issue, you need to practice effective listening, which requires focused attention and patience. Even with highly charged issues and large groups, it doesn't take long to hear out the thoughts and feelings of every participant. When there's no debate and participants aren't arguing or defending their points of view, you can hear from everyone in a brief amount of time.

No matter how urgent the situation or what pressure you may be feeling, it's worth the time and effort to be a reflective listener. It will put you on track with the real issue so that you can uncover effective solutions.

STEP #3 IN ACTION

Tough Issue: *Difficult Client Won't Stop Talking*

Mark, a contractor, had skyrocketing blood pressure. "I'm trying to finish a $500,000 construction project, and we're already more than $100,000 over estimate as a result of changes from my client Sam," he explained. "What's more, I can't get my work done because he keeps calling me about lots of little details. Our conversations can take up forty minutes or more. I want to be service-oriented and responsive, but I can't go on like this."

A Great Decision Solution

For Mark to get out of this dilemma with Sam, he needed to get to the essence of Sam's underlying feelings about the project. In other words, he needed to listen more deeply. This didn't come easily to Mark. "What do you mean, listen more deeply to what Sam is saying?" Mark asked. "The guy's already talking my ear off!" Since Sam talked so much, Mark had stopped listening. Not surprisingly, Sam talked even more because he sensed that Mark wasn't listening. Mark needed to break this vicious cycle.

After learning about Step #3, Mark asked Sam to tell him what he was thinking, and then he paraphrased Sam's thoughts. Before he answered what Sam said, Mark asked Sam to let him know if he had correctly summarized his feelings.

Sam talked, and Mark listened. Then Mark reflected the feelings he heard embedded in Sam's detailed questions: "It sounds like you've got many concerns about the project and what the changes are costing." "You're right," Sam answered. "I like the changes and feel good about your work. We can live with the new budget. But what can we do to keep on schedule and budget from here?"

Mark explained the overall plan for the remainder of the project. With his underlying concerns addressed, Sam stopped calling Mark so often, and the calls he did make were much shorter—usually only three to five minutes. Reflective listening not only got to the real issue but also made communications much more efficient. Furthermore, it increased client satisfaction, which is key for Mark's word-of-mouth referrals. Sam told his friends and colleagues, "That guy Mark really understands me."

THE KEYS TO STEP #3

Determine Whether the Presenting Issue Is the Real Issue

When an issue has festered for a long time, it's usually a sign that some other issue underlies it. For example, an upscale community had struggled for nearly a decade trying to decide whether to replace its crowded sixty-year-old elementary school. Two divisive school bond issue ballots had failed, and the outlook for any constructive action looked bleak.

On the face of it, the real issue seemed to be the need for a new school. Angry parents of schoolchildren bemoaned, "Our kids are stuffed into old classrooms like sardines. Teachers literally work out of closets. And we can't have a schoolwide event because even the gym isn't large enough. Don't the residents understand this? What's it going to take to resolve this situation?"

> *"The most important thing in communications is to hear what isn't being said."*
> —Peter Drucker

When business owners, educators, and residents were asked to talk about their thoughts and feelings regarding the school project, however, a different concern surfaced. As one person stated, "We're worried that the proposed school will stimulate growth that will strain our resources and alter the small-town character of our community." The real issue for many was not a new school but growth.

With the true issue in mind, residents were able to explore options for locating and building a new school that would not result in undesirable growth. They looked for sites closer to the town center and ones along existing transportation routes. The next school bond ballot sailed through with over 70 percent of the vote—an extraordinary landslide.

A similarly conflicted situation arose in a Silicon Valley church. Although it had a well-established congregation, including highly paid executives and successful entrepreneurs, it faced a budget crisis. Dozens of parishioners had come to meetings, and each person had offered a radically different idea about where to cut the budget. The arguments had become personal and intense. As one frustrated congregant said, "I can't believe that we're here in church and tearing away at each other. Can we solve this budget issue before we split apart?" Fear and the divisive dynamics that result from it can trouble any organization.

Certainly, the church had a significant budget problem. But as it turned out, that issue was not the core of the problem. Before sorting through all the proposed solutions, each person was asked to express his or her thoughts and concerns about the church and its budget. No debate was allowed, and no solutions could be championed. Church members could express anything they wanted as long as it was their own thoughts and feelings and not a judgment or an accusation about someone else.

Because forty-five people jammed into the meeting room for what was to be a brief meeting, they used a time-shaving shortcut. Each person wrote his or her thoughts and concerns on letter-size sheets of paper—one thought per sheet. When they finished writing, they posted the sheets on the wall and clustered similar thoughts and concerns together.

This exercise opened the floodgates. In minutes, dozens and dozens of sheets appeared on the wall. The largest cluster surrounded the theme of trust. For example, one person wrote, "There are some topics we need to discuss, but it doesn't feel OK to bring them up." And another said, "People in the congregation don't understand or trust me. They question my motives. I can't share my thoughts easily."

Since it was so clear that trust was actually the big issue, all the participants agreed to turn to that topic and discuss ways to restore trust. Having identified the real issue, they followed Steps #4 through #10 to explore the options and select appropriate courses of action to strengthen their community.

Several months later, the church leader proudly reported the results: "We no longer have a budget deficit. In fact, we have a sizeable surplus!" What had happened? She explained: "When people started trusting one another more, they began to participate in the church more actively. We stopped debating and started working together." As people participated more actively in the church, they opened their pocketbooks and also attracted new members.

These same dynamics can be applied in situations such as developing a new project with potential joint venture partners or raising capital for a business. If you don't know what the stakeholders consider to be the real issues, you can't make progress toward your goal. Reflective listening is a critical way for any organization to pinpoint the issues it needs to address in order to make great decisions that result in effective problem solving.

Listen for Feelings as Well as Content

Reflective listening also helps people solve problems themselves. When people have a chance to say what's on their minds and hear what they've said, they sometimes are able to resolve their own issues.

Remember Mark and Sam? Sam's many calls about the construction project frustrated Mark. When Mark asked Sam to tell him his thoughts, Mark was able to identify and address Sam's real concern. Beneath all the detailed questions about the job was the underlying concern about keeping the budget and schedule in line. Listening produced understanding, which decreased Sam's need to keep calling Mark.

Mirror What People Express

Some people discover what they think through speaking. My experience is that one-fourth or more of people in business and community situations do their thinking aloud, especially on emotionally charged issues. For example, they might say, "I'm really upset about this issue and don't know what to do. Can you listen to me for a few minutes?" Many people need others as a sounding board in order to clarify their own thinking.

When you work with people in this way, some may occasionally respond to your accurate paraphrasing of their thoughts and feelings by commenting, "I didn't say that—or, at least, that's not what I meant." If this happens, don't argue with them. Their thoughts are evolving. Simply offer your reflection of their revised comments and then check again to determine whether you have accurately captured their thoughts and concerns. (See Figure 8.)

Mirroring what someone says might seem as if it would take a lot of time. But effective listening is actually a tremendous timesaver. It is a technique for cutting to the chase and uncovering the real issue, and thus frees up time for the group to focus on that.

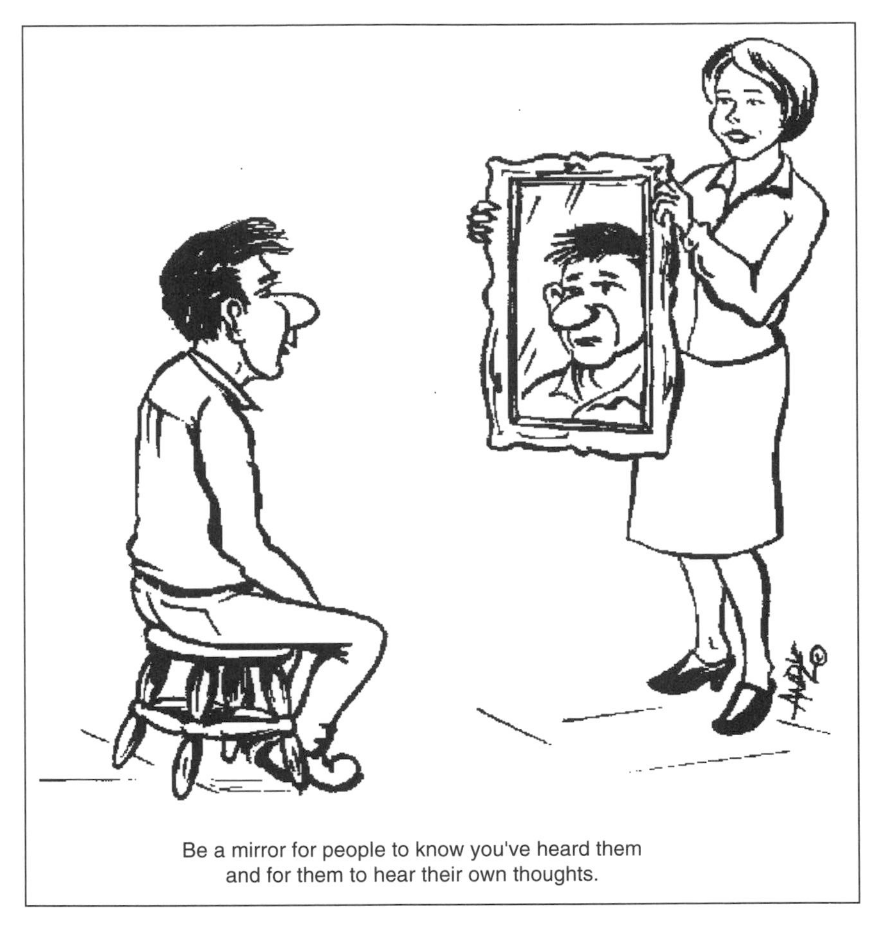

Be a mirror for people to know you've heard them
and for them to hear their own thoughts.

FIGURE 8 Accurately reflect thoughts and feelings.

Reflecting feelings, however, does require tact. Some people may not be open to examining their feelings or having others paraphrase them. In such cases, ask for permission: "May I reflect back what I think I'm hearing?" Remember, you're not trying to dictate to someone what he or she is feeling. You're just trying to reflect the feelings as expressed to you.

Sometimes a person's feelings conflict with what the person thinks. In this case, the person needs an opportunity to resolve the conflict before you can work together effectively. Adopt a lighter tone in such a situation. You don't want to shut the person down by being too heavy-handed in your reflection of what is being said. For example, your approach might be something like this: "I'm not sure, but it sounds like you're saying . . ."

No matter how wrongheaded or unjustified other people's thoughts and feelings may seem to you, don't edit them. When they hear themselves clearly, they will make the corrections themselves. The open discussion of options, along with their negatives and positives, that occurs in Steps #4 through #10 will also give people many opportunities to revise their thinking without a bruised ego.

Give Physical Form to Thoughts and Concerns

Some people resist expressing their thoughts or feelings. Perhaps they want to jump ahead to solutions, or maybe they aren't aware of any deeper thoughts and feelings than the relatively superficial issue in front of them.

In these cases, invite the relevant parties to depict their views physically. They could draw pictures of how they see the situation, Or they might act out the situation.

For example, an entrepreneur facing a tough organizational issue used a technique called *sculpting* suggested by Mark Bryan, author of *Artist's Way at Work: Riding the Dragon* (William Morrow, 1998). The entrepreneur and her team used volunteers to physically represent the feuding departments in the company. They arranged these people—like pieces of sculptor's clay—to depict how the departments interacted. Her business "sculpture" showed the hand-off between design and production and the rub points between sales and finance. After seeing how out of balance the current business sculpture was and hearing from the actors about how it physically felt for them to be in their positions, the team had a fresh perspective on their issues. Through the playful spirit of the business sculpture, they could demonstrate issues that were difficult to express.

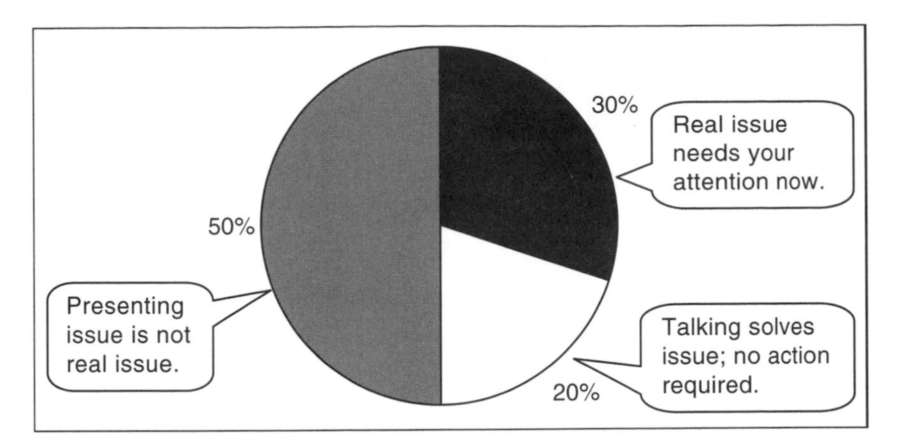

FIGURE 9 Find the real issue.

Try finding inventive ways to explore the important issues you face.

Target Your Attention Where It Counts

If you take the time needed to listen and learn what the real issue is, you can whittle away the presenting issues and focus on the critical issue that needs immediate attention. Let the involved parties talk out the issues they can solve on their own. What's left will be the real issue that needs attention now in order to achieve the desired result. This targeted issue may constitute only a fraction of all the issues that face you (see Figure 9), but targeting your attention saves time and energy and prepares you for the remainder of the decision process.

PUTTING STEP #3 INTO PRACTICE

1. *Step aside from problem solving. Instead, focus on issue finding.* Don't let the rush to solve a problem distract you from uncovering the real issue. Allow enough time for the power of listening to work.

2. *Ask all participants to express their thoughts and feelings in turn.* Include feelings, dreams, and other concerns, because the real issues often reside at these deeper levels. Encourage group participants to express themselves without the need to edit their statements and without fear of ridicule from others.

3. *Use "I" statements to avoid judging others.* Express what you think or feel from your own perspective without making assumptions about other people's motivations. Instead of falling into the pattern of saying, "You [made me angry or caused a problem], say instead, "I [felt angry or noticed a result] when [something occurred]."

4. *Listen without leaping to debate or solutions.* Allow statements to be no more and no less than what they are—thoughts and feelings from someone's perspective. When participants take ownership of their thoughts and feelings and don't judge others, they can say almost anything without harming someone else.

5. *Reflect back what you hear. Don't editorialize.* Express the spirit of what someone says. Don't agree or disagree—just be a mirror. This will free you from having to evaluate or judge anyone's statements. If there are multiple participants, ask the next person to speak to do the reflecting before beginning his or her own statement. You want to be sure that everyone is listening rather than preparing a speech.

   You've probably encountered people who keep repeating the same message to the same people. When you listen clearly and completely to people and demonstrate that you have truly heard their message, you can break that cycle.

6. *Ask the speaker whether you have accurately reflected what he or she wanted to say.* Sometimes, what people say is not what they mean. In fact, some people discover what they think only as they speak. When you reflect back what you've heard, you

give people an opportunity to modify or restate their perspectives.

7. *Identify the underlying issue that the group needs to address now.* Let the statements settle. Invite participants to express the themes they heard. The real issue will bubble to the top.

BE AN AGENT OF HOPE

Be a mirror, not a sponge. Many hard feelings arise and decision-making efforts derail because people absorb what they think others said and meant without checking it out first. It's much easier, more effective, and less painful to be a mirror rather than a sponge. Discover the real issue that needs immediate attention.

STEP #4

Identify All Options

See the Whole Tree Before You Go out on a Limb

The best way to have a good idea
is to have lots of ideas.
—Linus Pauling

Before you evaluate particular solutions to a problem, you need to get all options out on the table. Unfortunately, many groups begin with too few options. Some make up their minds after considering only one idea.

Western culture values finding an answer and finding it quickly. We want to appear knowledgeable. People in positions of responsibility particularly fear appearing unprepared. They want to have answers and be able to justify why they are in charge.

Education and training don't necessarily overcome these primal urges. For example, in the medical field, some physicians order many fruitless medical tests and appear to follow a hit-or-miss treatment strategy. However, other physicians get to an accurate diagnosis and treatment plan more quickly and effectively.

In the late 1980s I led a venture investment team looking for opportunities to improve physician effectiveness. Our mission was to learn how we could boost the performance of the average physician to be more like that of the top 20 percent of physicians. If we could discover how to do that, we believed we could save billions of dollars from wasted diagnostic tests and ineffective treatments.

Our inquiries indicated that a substantial percentage of physicians made preliminary diagnoses of their patients within a few moments of meeting them. On that basis, they proceeded to order tests or initiate treatments to prove or disprove their initial assessment. When one route failed, they'd start down another. No wonder so many patients became frustrated and health care costs soared.

In contrast, top-performing physicians took time when they first met their patients to consider several alternative possibilities before pursuing tests or treatments for any one of them. Top-performing doctors didn't necessarily have more knowledge or training. Instead, they had a process to consider multiple options before pursuing costly and time-consuming courses of action.

To be a good doctor in your business, you need to identify a full set of choices before you launch into a solution. Choices give you strength because they free you from being locked into the boxes of conventional thought.

STEP #4 IN ACTION

Tough Issue: *Intermittent Breakdowns Cost Millions*

The team at a forty-year-old power plant faced a multi-million-dollar problem. "Twice in the last three weeks," explained Mike, the plant manager, "the 37-ton rotor on one of the turbines has fallen out of alignment. Both incidents required an emergency shutdown. Spinning at 3,600 revolutions per minute, an out-of-alignment rotor can destroy tens of millions of dollars of equipment in minutes. But taking the unit out of service will cost our company a million dollars a day to purchase the power elsewhere."

The maintenance supervisor for the unit felt confident that he had the solution. "We know this machine," he commented. "I want to take the unit down and start work immediately."

Mike wasn't so sure. It was a tricky problem because it occurred intermittently. Since the metal expanded as the temperature rose to 1,000 degrees and no one could look inside the rotor enclosure while the turbine operated, everything was speculation. With millions of dollars riding on any decision, everyone needed to understand what was going on and to consider their options carefully.

A Great Decision Solution

Mike began by inviting a broad range of people to a meeting (Step #1). In addition to the maintenance supervisor and members of his department, the group included operators for the unit as well as plant engineers.

Next, all the participants reviewed the hopes they had previously developed together (Step #2). They recalled their commitment to teamwork and their hope of being the benchmark plant in their industry. This step reminded them that they wanted to avoid the interdepartmental rivalries that had plagued them in the past.

Then the operators described the operating conditions during which the problems occurred, what the gauges showed, and how the vibrations felt. The maintenance personnel discussed what they did at the last maintenance cycle for the unit and how the rotor looked at that time. The plant engineers showed schematics for the unit and printouts of the diagnostic tests they'd run. (This completed Step #3.)

Now they put Step #4 into practice. Since nearly twenty people participated and had widely varying levels of knowledge and experience with the unit, everyone wrote down solution options on sheets of paper and posted them on the wall. The participants were told they wouldn't have to defend any particular idea; they just needed to get them out.

In a short amount of time, the group had spread more than forty sheets of paper across the wall and clustered them into about a dozen different alternatives—ten times more possibilities than had surfaced before this step. The ideas ranged from an immediate shutdown and replacement of a suspected subassembly to a complete overhaul of the rotor unit. The team also included the status quo approach (close monitoring of the turbine but not yet making repairs) so that they could assess whether or not to make a change.

In the course of the two-hour meeting, the team accomplished several important tasks concerning the options:

1. They discussed each one so that everyone was clear about what it meant.

2. They checked how the options fit with the information they had and agreed upon a list of four key options.

3. They identified sources of information to evaluate the options further.

This step got the team working together to find a more effective solution than the maintenance supervisor's original idea. The ultimate solution turned out to be a totally new approach—one that they hadn't considered before taking this step. The insights they shared identified ways to operate the unit that lessened the likelihood of breakdowns. Thus, they kept the unit in operation while planning a targeted repair at a less critical time. Proud of his team, the plant manager reported, "Our investment in exploring new options got us on a path to a superior result that saved us a significant amount of time and money."

THE KEYS TO STEP #4

Identify Options with an Open Mind

The way you bring alternatives to the surface makes a big difference in the possibilities you come up with. All too often, participants in a group or meeting focus on advocating their own ideas, attacking others' ideas, or withholding potential solutions to avoid the fray. Such fear-based responses stifle the possibility of discovering creative solutions to the problem at hand.

If the only tool you have is a hammer,
you tend to see every problem as a nail.
—Abraham Maslow

In order to shift to a positive, hopeful approach and get the best results from the decision-making process, participants must keep their egos free from attachment to particular options and remain open to new possibilities. They need to feel free to shift their stance from position advocacy to idea generation without fear of others judging their ideas prematurely.

Use Catalysts to Precipitate New Ideas

People learn and explore ideas in multiple ways. In addition to visual sources (such as schematics and instruction books), auditory means (such as hearing the sound of a machine part or listening to others' ideas) and physical movement (such as acting out a scenario) can yield valuable insights and potential solutions. Explore all three modes to increase the likelihood of finding innovative solutions to your problems.

One of the stimuli for the turbine plant team's creative ideas came from an unconventional approach. Since no one could see inside the turbine rotor assembly, and the diagrams offered an abstract view, volunteers used their bodies to act out what they thought the units were doing when the breakdowns occurred. They lined up in the conference room, with different people taking different positions, and simulated how the long, complex chain of pieces moved and changed under different conditions. This kinesthetic enactment helped the group apprehend the problem in a fresh way and identify several new ideas.

People have many more ideas and possibilities in their heads than they typically consider. Often, the pieces are there, and they simply need a catalyst for new solutions to form. Use trigger concepts or metaphors to precipitate inventive approaches. The bibliography at the back of this book identifies several resources to stimulate new ideas.

Look at the Whole Tree to Get Fruitful Results

Think of your problem as a tree with many branches. Look at the whole tree and all the branches you could follow before you go out on a particular limb. (See Figure 10.) You'll get more fruitful results more quickly.

Explore all of the options to find the most fruitful results.

FIGURE 10 See the whole tree before you go out on a limb.

Turn Challenges into Opportunities

After a team penetrates to the bedrock of its hopes, it can tap a broad array of potential solutions. Liberated from preconceived avenues to realizing their hopes, team members can explore new options. When they have many choices, participants in a decision-making group don't feel trapped or forced into a particular course of action. Having choices unleashes new energy.

PUTTING STEP #4 INTO PRACTICE

1. *Stimulate new ideas.* Our minds can seize the opportunity to realign our thinking. Use catalysts—concepts that trigger new ways of thinking, word pictures that describe a situation from analogous perspectives, and physical movement—to open up fresh options.

2. *Invite each person to state one option in turn.* After each member of your group has had time to reflect about options, begin the process by having someone mention one. Proceed to the next person and so on through the group, inviting each participant to offer a different option. Encourage new ideas.

   The only criterion for mentioning an option is that the person thinks the option might help the group pursue its hopes for resolving the issue in question. Stating an option at this stage doesn't commit the presenter to supporting it. If any particular individual cannot come up with an option that has not already been mentioned, the person should pass. Repeating options only provides redundant information and discourages additional ideas.

   Have each person offer only one option on each circle around the group. This gives more participants a chance to offer possible solutions. Remember, it's not who comes up with an idea that counts; it's how many good ideas you can generate and how involved participants become in finding those ideas that determine success.

3. *Avoid debate or comments. Stick to an open brainstorming approach.* This is not the time to evaluate options. Debate discourages people from offering original and untried ideas. You'll identify each option's positives and negatives later on, in Step #6.

4. *Expand your perspectives playfully.* As you brainstorm, encourage logical thoughts (left brain), creative thoughts (right brain), and deep senses (gut feelings). Find ways to give expression to intuition. For example, draw pictures of the options or imagine what each might say if it could talk. Have some fun as you proceed. It will lighten the work and open the process to new ideas.

   What do your gut-level feelings suggest? As I learned in the early 1990s when I was developing a company seeking improved treatments for migraine headaches, the neuroreceptors in our intestines share similarities with those in our brains. There is an intelligence in gut feelings that's worth understanding.

5. *Continue brainstorming until all options have been offered.* Proceed around the group, with each person offering a new option, until all participants have expressed all their ideas. This may take several rounds. Encourage participants to identify other options, even if someone has already mentioned their own favored solutions. When they express options from outside their own preset point of view, they loosen their attachment to specific outcomes and begin the process of identifying with new possibilities.

   If, after going around the group, all you end up with are the options you started with, dig deeper. But don't worry if you end the meeting with the feeling that you haven't assembled a complete set of options. Later steps in the decision-making process will help you uncover new possibilities.

6. *List all viable options, from the status quo to the more adventuresome, that are worthy of further investigation.* After your brain-

storming, decide which of the options merit further consideration. If you are unsure about whether to evaluate an option, include it on your list. It won't take your group very long to assess it, and including it ensures that no one's option is eliminated prematurely. Be inclusive of diverse options at the start, which will increase buy-in for the final choices your group makes.

Unless the current situation is untenable, include the status quo in your list of options. After all, this is what you are currently doing. Including it as an option helps you understand why you are doing it. Many groups falter in their efforts to take new directions because they don't thoroughly examine their current activities. Consequently, some people remain attached to the way things are, but others bound ahead. Great decisions get everyone on board to move ahead together.

BE AN AGENT OF HOPE

Scout for fresh ideas. Choices give you strength to look at issues more creatively. Encourage everyone to identify multiple options in order to find the most fruitful results.

STEP #5

Gather the Right Information

Look Through the Lens of Your Hopes

The fog of information can drive out knowledge.
—Daniel Boorstin

Step #5 integrates the results of the previous steps. Step #1 yielded a broad and balanced working group whose members share a commitment to proceed with open minds. Step #2 identified the members' underlying hopes and aspirations. Step #3 sharpened the issues of importance to examine. Step #4 guided members to identify innovative options.

Step #5 helps group members gather the information they need to choose the best solution from among the options they've generated. Ineffective information gathering plagues many groups dealing with tough issues. Although the participants espouse shared objectives, they readily tend to fall back into old patterns of factional dynamics as they proceed. The upshot of this is that they unnecessarily create adversaries and fail to reach effective agreements.

Corporations have their own institutional biases. For example, when a tough issue arises that concerns a struggling product, a manager will often react by sending marketing off to gather information about customer demand, asking operations to analyze the requirements for delivering the product, and directing finance to run the numbers on the investment and its returns. This type of "silo" thinking may leverage each group's expertise and align with the organization's functional structure, but it also reinforces imbalances and adversarial behavior. The finance group might show up with reams of spreadsheets to validate its skepticism of marketing's statistics. The operations group might fail to see why it needs to make product changes and, therefore, resist finding a creative solution for retooling the production line. Such oppositional dynamics often work at subtle levels. They can be so deeply engrained in the corporate culture that workers take them for granted or fail to recognize that they exist.

Another difficulty with functional or interest-driven information gathering is that often people collect only information that is readily available or that others have gathered. When they don't screen the information on the basis of how it relates to their own objectives, they tend to collect either too much or too little information or they don't gather what they really need. Those engaged in information gathering need a clear organizing principle to aid them.

Issues that are allowed to fester may signify the presence of an information gap. In this case, participants and decision makers lack the understanding they need to find and implement an effective solution to the problem being considered. For example, a reorganization may show strong financial returns, but until those involved in it grasp the implications of how they will work together within the new structure, there's little support for its implementation.

The method that groups employ to gather information dramatically affects their problem-solving results. Although interest-driven approaches to collecting data can be effective ways to get day-to-day work accomplished, solving tough issues for the long term requires a better approach—one based on the shared hopes of the group's participants.

STEP #5 IN ACTION

Tough Issue: *Deeply Divided Interests Try to Work Together*

Business leaders, educators, taxpayer groups, and parents agreed to tackle the overcrowding issues at their elementary school. (See the example in Step #3.) Following the ten-step process, the task force enlisted a wide range of people, discovered their shared hopes, uncovered the real issues, and identified a number of options for resolving the overcrowding problem, including the status quo solution of doing nothing. Many people on the team held strong opinions about which solution was best.

Then it was time to gather information about all the possible options. Since there was too much for everyone to do together, they needed to divide up the work. "Let's set up separate groups to gather information about each option and report back," suggested one team member. Other volunteers on the community team nodded in agreement. Why not let each person work on the option he or she preferred?

Fortunately, Daphne, one of the volunteers, spoke up. "Hey, if we form a separate information-gathering group for each option, we will simply divide ourselves into the old factions. That won't help us find a solution that fulfills our shared hopes." Daphne valued the understanding and goodwill the group had generated through the previous steps and didn't want to see it lost.

A Great Decision Solution

Daphne knew in her gut that researching and defending positions in factions would lead to a dead end. "We've been down that route many times over the years and have gotten nowhere," she commented. "If we do it that way again, I can see that most people will simply follow the option they preferred at the start. Why would they choose any differently? There would be nothing to encourage them to consider different points of view."

The team agreed to gather information based on the three hopes its members shared: educational quality, cost-effectiveness, and neutral growth. One group examined all of the options from the perspective of how they would fulfill the objective of educational quality. This group included educators with relevant expertise as well as residents who had been skeptical of the need for a new facility. Another team including both planners and concerned taxpayers, pursued the hope of a cost-effective solution. These participants delved into the projected costs for each option and compared them with similar projects. A third team pursued the hope of being growth-neutral, a hope that surfaced in the community's discussion of thoughts and concerns as they followed Step #3. This group researched how each option would help the community live within its resources. It included environmentalists and school administrators as part of the team.

By using their shared hopes to focus their information gathering, the task force came up with an efficient way to obtain all the facts they needed to find outstanding solutions to the problem of overcrowded schools and the support to implement them. Each work group reported on how the different options supported a hope they all shared. The experience of working together toward a common objective helped the fractious interests move forward together. They made the transition from being advocates to learners. This was a critical development in the process of achieving a decision with broad support. (You'll learn more about their results in Step #7.)

THE KEYS TO STEP #5

Use Hopes to Focus Information Gathering

The process of resolving tough issues that confront business or community organizations requires focused information. Shared hopes can guide you to find the right information—the information that relates to your important objectives. (See Figure 11.)

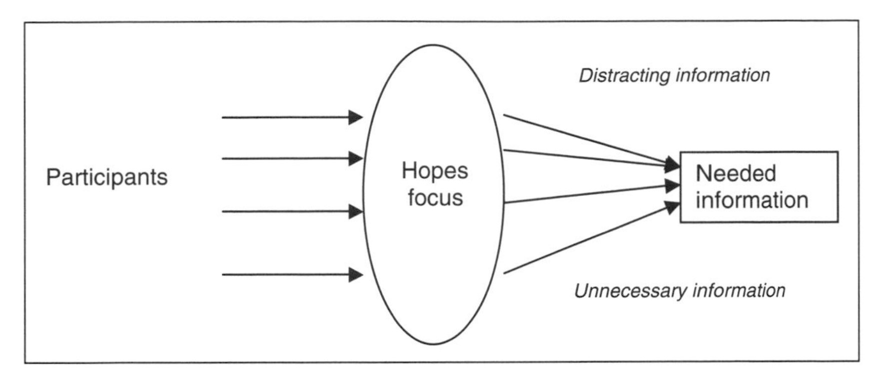

FIGURE 11 Look through the lens of your hopes.

Focused information gathering can help you avoid the "paralysis of analysis" that comes from coping with a distracting fog of information. The typical approach to information gathering is to pull together all of the information that is available on the issue in question and then attempt to examine it. Such an "exhaustive" analysis may yield nothing more than that—exhaustion. Other groups give up before they start, in despair about not having enough time to analyze all of the information and reach a solution. However, if you filter your information through the core set of hopes—what's really important—you'll have the time for analysis and the process will be efficient.

Looking through the lens of your hopes also ensures that participants seek out critical information that they might otherwise miss. It shifts the focus from "What information do we have?" to "What information do we need?" Soft data on intangibles, such as how the options will affect educational quality or growth in the community, receive balanced consideration with more easily quantified and accessible information about capital investment and operating costs.

Present Information but Don't Present Conclusions

When you have gathered information for a group presentation, convey the information as accurately as possible without making conclusions or offering recommendations. If you interpret the facts or advocate a particular conclusion, others will think you are biased and discount your information.

For example, participants on the school task force (see Step #3) heard from all three groups and weighed the negatives and positives of each option (see Step #6) before they reached an informed point of view. This stepwise approach built credibility and established buy-in for their ultimate decision.

Gathering information without bias is also beneficial in another regard. Freed from advocacy roles, group members can efficiently gather facts without fretting over the implications of any particular fact. Because they know multiple factors will weigh into the conclusions, they can be inclusive in their data gathering without fear.

Encourage Shared Experiences

When group members work as a team, openly and sensitively, they're able to share the wider concerns of their colleagues and other stakeholders. For example, because the school task force members heard feedback from the broader community in Step #3, they knew what was of particular concern to people and were able to explore the broad issues on everyone's behalf.

Sharing hopes and experiences also brings people closer together. Although many participants had been involved on one side or the other of the school overcrowding issue for years, when they began using the ten-step process, it was the first time some of them had ever actually worked together. As they gathered facts about the different options, physically visiting potential school sites, poring over cost estimates, and examining growth issues together, they shared experiences and gained mutual understanding.

An added advantage is that open and balanced information gathering contributes to the overall credibility of the decision-making process. Participants trust that an unbiased process yields useful information without needing to explore every item themselves.

HOPES AID EFFECTIVE INFORMATION GATHERING BY:

- Efficiently focusing attention on what's important
- Clearly defining types of information to consider
- Maintaining balanced perspectives among participants
- Encouraging shared learning
- Building understanding and support for effective solutions

PUTTING STEP #5 INTO PRACTICE

1. *Use your hopes to focus your information gathering.* What do you want to accomplish and why? Orient your information gathering around the way each option supports your hopes.

   An easy way to focus your efforts is to create a table with the options you are considering listed in the left-hand column and the key hopes you want to realize arrayed as headings across the top of the other columns. Then, enter information about how each option relates to each of your hopes. (See Table 3.) This structured approach will keep your information gathering focused and balanced. It will also overcome any organizational biases.

2. *Avoid setting up factional dynamics and advocating particular positions.* Unfortunately, many groups set themselves up for divisive failures. Participants work only on the options they like and then battle it out with each other. This process reinforces their ego attachments to specific approaches and diminishes the opportunity for creative solutions that can earn broad support. By pursuing information and results through shared

TABLE 3 Gather Information Based on Your Hopes

Organize your information-gathering groups according to your key hopes. For each hope, gather information about how the options support it. Use your hopes to guide your information gathering.

OPTIONS	HOPE A	HOPE B	HOPE C	HOPE D
Option 1	[How does Option 1 fulfill Hope A?]	[How does Option 1 fulfill Hope B?]		
Option 2	[How does Option 2 fulfill Hope A?]			
Option 3				
Option 4				
Option 5				

hopes, your team can avoid the unpleasantness and inefficiency of factional fighting.

3. *Include a variety of participants to strengthen learning.* View information gathering as a learning process for the whole group, rather than as an expertise-driven way to get things done. For example, don't put all the financial people in one group and all the marketing people in another. You need enough experts in each work group, but you also want others to learn about areas of concern outside their own specialty. Including participants from a variety of areas and with wide-ranging experiences will build a broader, cross-linked foundation for surfacing new ideas, exploring fresh opportunities, bridging differences, and reaching agreement.

4. *Learn relevant information from others.* How have others addressed similar issues? If you learn how different groups approached making their decision, you may not have to reinvent the wheel. The critical thing is to find others with similar hopes and circumstances; be sure that the examples you study are in alignment with your group's particular hopes. It won't help to follow someone else's map if it doesn't lead you where you want to go.

5. *Be focused, not exhaustive.* Get just enough information to make a first cut on how each of the options addresses your key hopes. Some groups expend so much effort gathering information that they are exhausted before they even start to evaluate what they've learned. Reserve time and energy for new, creative ideas that emerge or to refine the options that appear most appealing.

BE AN AGENT OF HOPE

Use your shared hopes as a lens to focus all of your activities. Structure your working groups and information gathering according to them. Whenever you sense that you're getting lost in the fog, return to your shared hopes as a simple yet highly effective organizing principle.

STEP #6

Get Everything on the Table

100 Percent Information, Zero Percent Debate

This same progeny of evils comes
From our debate, from our dissension.
—William Shakespeare

If debates are raging in your business or organization, you are wasting time and money. You're also destroying the goodwill needed to make great decisions and realize outstanding results.

Western culture has mistakenly elevated debating to a high art form. We have debate clubs, debating societies, and even debates to help select among political candidates. But debate is a dead end for getting things done.

Staking out positions and squaring off in verbal duels have high costs:

1. *Debate polarizes positions.* Rather than having everyone search for the best option together, debate forces each side to advocate its own case. This resembles the ancient gladiator battles. The emphasis is on making points and winning rather than on finding the best solution.

   Remember how the operations and maintenance groups at the industrial plant bickered before they began the ten-step process? (See the example in Step #2.) When problems arose, the finger-pointing began. The operators complained that the maintenance department didn't keep the unit in good repair. Maintenance charged that the operators pushed the equipment too far. As the debates ensued, the ego stakes rose. Who was right? Who was wrong? Whose career would advance? Whose would suffer? Meanwhile, problems festered without the benefit of the best thinking that could come about only when both groups worked together.

2. *Debate hides rather than discloses important information.* Were you ever part of a high school debate team? I remember preparing for my high school debates by filling index cards with the key points supporting my position. I also anticipated opposing points of view and had facts, figures, and expert opinions to rebut them. The game was to make the best case for my position and hope that the other person didn't score on my areas of vulnerability. In fact, I often knew the weaknesses of my position better than my opponent. But it wasn't my role to disclose all of the facts. My role was to win.

   The same is true in many organizations. It's not that people can't see the bigger picture. Rather, it's that the process people use to decide issues doesn't encourage it. Advocates know the dark underside of their positions, but because they fear losing, they don't disclose all that they know, even though it would help find superior solutions.

3. *Even the "winners" lose.* With the passage of time and some perspective, it's clear that most gladiator-style victories are short-lived. The losers in corporate power struggles or public elections regroup and continue their battles to regain "face." The victories are fragile because they lack commitment to shared success. Meanwhile, organizations and communities suffer from suboptimal decisions or decision gridlock.

Winners and losers do not make good learners.

Debating is a good game but a bad model for sorting out issues with other people. In business, the highest purpose isn't to see who wins but to build the best results together. We need to separate egos from issues in order to get great results.

It's time to recognize debate for the fear-driven dynamic that it is and adopt a better process for resolving tough issues. It's time to say *no* to debate.

STEP #6 IN ACTION

Tough Issue: *Future Products for a Billion-Dollar Company*

Tim, an R&D manager at a Fortune 500 company, worried that the discussion of alternatives for his company's next generation of products would be like walking into the full force of a storm. (See the description of Tim's group in Part 1.) "This is where we could fall back into the old dynamics of debate and one-upmanship," he feared. "I don't want another meeting in which participants feud endlessly with no results. We need to be able to get our perspectives out on the table in a respectful and constructive way."

A Great Decision Solution

When it came time to discuss the company's alternatives, the members of Tim's team began by reading the shared hopes they had developed earlier, recalling the larger purpose of their efforts. Next, they examined the option of the current software platform by going from person to person to hear everyone's negatives or perceived product limitations. Each person stated only one negative at a time to avoid the kind of dynamics that had reigned in the past, in which members had gone off on extended diatribes. The new procedure also gave each person an opportunity to express a perspective and maintain a personal balance about the option. All members understood that stating a negative didn't mean they necessarily opposed the option under consideration. It simply acknowledged the reality that the option had shortcomings.

Group members didn't repeat a negative that someone had already stated. Had they done so, they would have been providing redundant information, creating the impression that the momentum was swinging in a particular direction.

The guidelines also precluded debate about whether what someone stated was truly a negative. A few participants bridled at this constraint. They prided themselves on letting nothing slip by their critical review. But it was exactly this combative behavior that had put people on edge in their group and stymied decision making and the collective results that they needed.

If someone stated a negative but someone else thought it was a positive, the second person was expected to wait to mention it until it was time to state the positives, which was the next part of this step. This approach doesn't preclude any input but simply structures it so that everyone can receive information more constructively. Debate tactics put the speaker on the defensive, but this approach allows everyone to absorb information without the distortion of ego attachments or defenses. Then, when it comes time to choose an option in Step #7, they can change their minds without losing face.

After cycling through the team members a couple of times, they exhausted all of the negatives about the status quo option. The team then went through the same process for the positives about the status quo, enumerating how the current software supported their shared hopes. Several positive attributes emerged, and participants kept those in mind as they considered subsequent options.

Why present the negatives about an option before the positives? The simple answer is that it works better. The shortcomings of an option or plan typically carry more force than its positives. Perhaps our fears or worries are more dominant than our hopes. When participants get the negatives out on the table, it's easier for them to think of the positives.

The software researchers proceeded to explore two new options in less than an hour, following the same process as they did for the status quo option. How did it go? Here are some of their comments:

> "I like how each option received a fair hearing."
>
> "I felt we each acknowledged the benefits and shortcomings for our choices."
>
> "What a relief to get everything on the table without divisive debates."

The process was a success.

As it has with dozens of groups, Step #6 redirected the participants' competitive instincts from debating to providing information about the negatives and positives of each option. The process didn't sublimate the urge to score points. Instead, it scored them for the team's benefit rather than at the expense of other members.

Tough Issue: *Developing an Organizational Growth Plan with Many Players*

"We're growing fast, starting new initiatives, and need to plan how we're going to organize ourselves for the future," explained Alex, the leader of nationally recognized firm. "I want to bring all of the field staff from our various sites together, along with the central office staff and members of our board. We're blessed with a creative and talkative group. The concern is how to hear from each of the thirty-five participants, avoid having a few long-winded members dominate the conversation, and reach some preliminary conclusions in the course of an afternoon meeting."

A Great Decision Solution

Alex had lots of insights and experience. He was a veteran of McKinsey & Company, the elite international consulting firm, and an organizational expert before starting up his new business. Nonetheless, he faced the realities of finding ways to involve team members and make timely decisions, just like everyone else.

Following Step #6 brought Alex the results he wanted. Similar to the R&D team previously described, Alex's team went through the process of defining the negatives and the positives of all the options they identified. The members examined the alternatives of centralizing and decentralizing key responsibilities as they explored how to grow and retain their innovative culture. Since the organization relied heavily upon personal initiative as well as a shared direction, each participant had important perspectives to share about the choices.

This step gave them a double win. "The team members not only laid out the negatives and positives of all of the initial options," Alex raved, "but also came up with some promising new approaches that no one had thought of before. And we didn't even have to work hard at it. Listening openly to the strengths and weaknesses of each option prompted even better ideas for how to organize ourselves. This step is both efficient and effective!"

THE KEYS TO STEP #6

Focus on a 100 Percent Information Exchange

To get the most out of Step #6, flip the standard debating approach on its head. Don't even let a debate begin. If you follow this guideline, each person will be able to express negatives as well as positives about each option under consideration. No one will be able to dominate the discussion to favor his or her point of view. Everyone's best thinking will have a chance to air without needless repetition or debate.

However, in order to accomplish a successful information exchange, you must follow Step #6 carefully. It can be difficult for people to listen to something negative about an idea they favor. It can be even more difficult for them to say something positive about ideas they don't like. Group members must agree to adhere to the established structure so that they can feel confident that everyone is playing by the same rules and not taking advantage of the open-minded atmosphere.

Using this step for information exchange enabled a regional government agency to turn around a difficult budget confrontation. Its board of directors needed to slash millions of dollars from its already lean operating budget. "If we approach this like a typical issue, with each member making speeches and advocating and debating positions, we'll be at each other's throats," the board president commented. "We need a way to work through this issue that gets results and also demonstrates to community members that we've all heard their concerns, assessed the relevant considerations, and reached thoughtful conclusions."

The board applied Step #6 in their process of addressing the budget issue. Board members exchanged information about more than a dozen potential budget cuts in a cable-broadcast public meeting. The seven-member board completed the work in a little over an hour.

"If it hadn't been for this process, we would have been here for days," the board president reported. "What's more, both the public and the press have seen us at our best—thoughtfully sharing information. The cuts won't be popular, but at least everyone knows we each considered all the information openly."

Because the process for information exchange incorporated into this step is so open, it self-corrects for bias. It would be immediately apparent if someone close-mindedly advocated only one particular position. The other participants would recognize that the person had only positive things to say for his or her favored option and negative statements about the others. Because such bias manifests itself so obviously and runs counter to the group's shared hopes, participants restrain themselves from exhibiting such behavior, thereby avoiding the posturing that is typical of debate-oriented decision processes.

A particular advantage of Step #6 is that it helps even large groups address a broad range of options in a focused amount of time. This makes it feasible to include a large group of representative stakeholders and information providers, as outlined in Step #1, and still get the job done.

Develop New Options from What You've Learned

The hallmark of a learning organization and a successful decision-making process is that new and more effective options arise from the discussion. When Alex's team laid out the negatives and the positives of all their potential solutions, they not only considered all of them equally but also came up with several new options that no one had thought of previously. By thoroughly exploring all sides of every possibility and really listening to what others have to say, participants often generate new and exciting ideas.

Take Advantage of the Huge Improvement Potential

If your organization hasn't employed Step #6 yet, you're not alone. In a survey of middle managers from three dozen organizations representing a wide range of industries and small to large employee groups, few knew about or regularly applied this approach (see Appendix A). In fact, less than one-third regularly use a structured approach to air the pros and cons on major issues. However, when survey respondents were introduced to the ten steps, Step #6 was one of the most frequently cited ways to significantly improve their organizations.

PUTTING STEP #6 INTO PRACTICE

1. *Use your shared hopes as the basis for evaluation.* Before evaluating the first of your options, reflect on the hopes you share as a group for resolving the issue you face. When participants look at the bigger picture and consider the desired outcome for the group, they provide deeper and more useful insights.
2. *Begin with the status quo option before proceeding to the more adventuresome options.* Work through the list of options you devel-

oped in Step #4, but evaluate the status quo option first—this will be your benchmark for considering your other options. The process of exchanging statements about the negatives and positives of participants' current experience, and the level of understanding that results, can be a springboard for new directions.

3. *Start with the option's negative points.* Ask each person to express a different negative statement about the option under consideration. Proceed around the group in this way until all possible negatives have been stated for the option. Anyone who doesn't come up with a statement that hasn't already been mentioned should pass. Repetition of information allows cliques to form, which lead to adversarial dynamics.

   Be sure to start with the negatives about an option, because most people are better able to consider positives after stating the negatives. Encourage people who favor a particular option to participate in expressing its negatives. Often, they know its shortcomings better than anyone else.

4. *Instruct everyone to listen to what the others say without questioning or debating.* Even if there is disagreement about someone's negative statement, participants should acknowledge and accept it as that person's point of view. After hearing differing points of view, people are apt to revise their thinking. You don't need to agree with someone else's specific reasons to reach agreement on a shared course of action.

   The more contentious the issue, the more important it is to avoid debate. Remember that winners and losers make poor learners. Be alert for the wisdom that can be shared by means of this sort of information exchange.

5. *Then state the positives about the option.* Follow the same guidelines and procedures you followed for expressing negatives, but have each person express a different positive about the option. Encourage naysayers to identify something positive.

Sometimes one participant will mention a positive that someone else stated as a negative. For example, an option for a new school facility required that transportation be available to reach the school—which some might consider a negative. On the flip side, the location offered safety advantages—a positive—because no one would walk to it along unsafe streets. It's acceptable if the same point shows up in both the negatives and the positives.

6. *Proceed to express the negatives and positives of each of the remaining options.* Use the same process for expressing negatives and positives about each of the other options. The structured discussion promotes balance and candor. Advocates of a particular option usually become more receptive to other options because they don't want to appear as if they're stacking the deck in favor of their own ideas.

7. *After hearing all of the negatives and positives for each of your initial options, invite suggestions for new alternatives.* The open expression of negatives and positives and the balanced participation of all group members frequently stimulate ideas for new options. Often something better arises than the choices you first considered. The discovery of new options is one of the rewards of the ten-step process and proof that it is creating distinctive value for your organization.

BE AN AGENT OF HOPE

Don't debate. This is a remnant of the dynamics based on fear. Instead, revel in the freedom and productive results that come from a respectful, insightful, and efficient exchange of information.

STEP #7

Write Down Choices That Support Shared Hopes

Take the Guesswork out of Decisions

The strongest principle of growth
lies in human choice.
—George Eliot

Many managers say that they want candid input from their team members, but they don't take the simple actions necessary to get it. Consequently, they don't learn what others think will work best, and team members lack full commitment for successful implementation of any given solution. They also fall prey to fears, egotism, and inaccuracies. Step #7 is a means to overcome all of these problems, and it enables team members to find the best solutions to the problem they are trying to solve.

STEP #7 IN ACTION

Tough Issue: *Picking the Best Idea*

As project manager for an important new product, Jenny had just completed a meeting with representatives from marketing, design, and production. They came together to make a final decision about a key aspect of the product. Where and how would customers access the product? Would the firm use distributors? Should they offer it direct through the Internet? Would partnering with an established player in the market and integrating the new product into that company's products be a good idea? Each of these choices had important implications for the work groups represented at the meeting.

After laying out the options and discussing the merits of each alternative, Jenny suggested what she thought would be a desirable course of action. A few participants nodded their heads in agreement. No one objected. Jenny concluded the meeting by saying, "Well, then, let's go forward."

There are many problems with Jenny's approach. Did she pick the best idea? Was it really the one everybody thought would work most effectively? Or did Jenny's rush to confirm her own assessment and demonstrate that she was in charge make her overconfident of her team's response? Moreover, did people's nodding and going along with the suggested direction mean that they had reflected on all the choices and thought the suggested approach was best? Did they have enough time to quietly reflect on the choices? And what criteria did Jenny and other team members use to make their choices? If some team members had thought other alternatives would be better, how would Jenny have known?

Those problems aren't all. If participants had actually thought that a different path would have been preferable, wouldn't the vigor of their commitment to the direction Jenny proposed be less than it should be? And wouldn't it be better for Jenny to know the group's real level of support right then, so she could address the concerns, consider other alternatives more carefully, or at least appreciate that motivation might become an issue?

The biggest question, however, is whether everyone agreed to the same thing. Even if they heard Jenny's words, did they interpret them the same way?

A GREAT DECISION SOLUTION

Jenny made many assumptions and guesses about an important decision. She didn't hear what everyone on her team had to say about it and didn't take the time to thoroughly explore the options. Not surprisingly, her team foundered as they tried to implement the solution and the solution itself didn't stick.

The next time around, when her team needed to make a major decision, Jenny implemented Step #7. The group began by following Steps #1 through #6: enlisting everyone, discovering their shared hopes, uncovering the real issue, identifying all the options, and getting everything on the table. Then, in order to take the guesswork out of their decision making, they each wrote down the choice they thought was most desirable and would meet their shared hopes best. Using secret ballots, they voted for the solution they thought would most benefit their business objectives. Jenny and her team took the guesswork out of finding and developing the best solutions.

THE KEYS TO STEP #7

Reflect on Shared Hopes as the Basis for Your Selection

Leaders and teams need to remain focused on their ultimate objectives: fulfilling the hopes they share for the opportunity. Without a set of common themes, participants will only be solo performers—they'll never become a great symphony.

A group's shared hopes need reinforcement. Otherwise, participants tend to drift back to their own agendas. When you work with diverse team members, it's a good idea to keep their shared hopes before them in written form. If they haven't reviewed them in a while, ask each participant to read out one hope in order from the list when you meet next.

People also need time to let their shared hopes sink in and for desirable choices to bubble up. Knee-jerk reactions often arise from peoples' fears or personal agendas. Many groups produce poor results because they rush to a decision without even a minute of quiet reflection. Not surprisingly, they end up with worn-out ideas because of their shortsighted thinking.

In contrast, connecting with what's important to fulfill your long-term success together may take a few moments of reflection. Give yourselves this time. You've spent a substantial amount of time identifying the negatives and positives of each of the options you've generated. Reserving a few minutes for each person to reflect on the group's shared hopes and how the options fit with them is another sound investment.

Some people are quick draws and want to shoot immediately. Others need time to get up to speed. It takes only a relatively short amount of time to enable everyone to move forward together.

Commit Preferred Choices to Writing

The simple act of writing down the choices each person believes will best fulfill the shared hopes of the group solves many problems. First, it prompts participants to clarify the choices. In about half of the groups I've facilitated, people have had questions about one or more of the various options, even at this late stage in the overall process. They've wanted to be certain about the details before writing down what they think would be best for the group. Because some people process information more effectively in writing than through speaking or hearing, writing provides a way for them to clarify their thoughts. The combination of verbal discussion and writing also improves participants' memory retention of the choices considered.

Second, writing down the options ensures that no one's thinking gets left out. Participants in typical group efforts commonly lament that they feel pressured to go along with the rest of group. They complain that they don't have a chance to express their own points of view before the group rushes to a decision. In contrast, when each person writes down preferred options, participants discover exactly what everyone thinks.

Finally, writing choices on slips of paper encourages commitment to the results. Participants are far less likely to renege on the conclusion.

Even when dealing with small issues, it's important for each person to write down his or her choice. Doing so lets everyone express a preference in a respectful and efficient manner—and the results stick.

Specify Multiple Choices to Broaden Solutions

In addition to acknowledging each person's first choice, it's important to find out what other choices would be acceptable, albeit less desirable, ways to fulfill the group's shared hopes. Few decisions, especially on tough issues, are cut and dried, with clear yes-or-no or a-or-b choices. With the successful completion of Steps #6 and #7, a team will have multiple choices to consider, as well as an appreciation of the nuances of each choice. They will also perceive that there can be several paths to successful problem-solving results. When participants specify both a best choice and all acceptable other choices, the group gains information about the entire solution spectrum.

Some people, however, fear that advocates of a particular course of action will refrain from listing alternate choices in order to boost their own partisan point of view. This is analogous to walking the high wire without a net: If something happens, there is no backup. Steps #1 through #6 have established a strong, shared foundation for problem solving, which should discourage group members from advocating only their first choice. If someone does try to skew the process, it will be evident when everyone sees the results in Step #8.

With multiple choices come strength and resilience. Everyone benefits from listing as many options as are acceptable and supportive of their objectives. As you'll see in Step #9, acceptable alternatives prepare groups to adapt to changing circumstances and to pursue superior solutions as they proceed.

Use Secret Ballots for Candid Insights

Confidentiality allows each person to assess the options without being subject to groupthink or coercion. It honors each person as an instrument of discernment, no matter how timid or vocal that person may be. Secret ballots provide a critical opportunity for participants to transform their thinking and come to breakthrough results.

In the example of the school overcrowding issue described in Step #5, use of secret ballots allowed participants to change their previously staked positions and find a common solution. The volunteer committee included advocates and opponents of the two school bond measures that had failed. Both groups had spent thousands of dollars to influence the elections and had supporters in the community who wanted their representatives to deliver their predetermined positions.

Before committee members wrote down their recommended choices for resolving the issue, they read their shared hopes aloud. This reiterated the group's commitment to a solution that responded to the core themes of quality education, cost-effectiveness, and neutral growth. After writing down their choices, they submitted their secret ballots.

The results from the secret ballots demonstrated overwhelming support for a new site and a less costly construction plan. Afterward, an ardent supporter of the prior school bond proposal approached a friend on the committee and asked, "Why wasn't the original school site we worked so hard on together your first choice?" The committee member replied, "Because it wasn't the choice that would best fulfill our shared hopes for the community. I needed to let go of our old position in order to find a solution that would work." The focus on shared hopes and the buffer supplied by secret balloting kept committee members from reverting to their old, unproductive agendas.

Secret balloting works even in large legislative bodies. Although many states require all final decisions to take place in public, with a record of each member's vote, secret balloting offers an effective straw poll that can highlight areas of agreement. Elected officials can express what they think is best for their constituents and learn what their colleagues think without staking a final position. It offers them the opportunity to explore possibilities without fear of being left to twist alone in the wind.

Secret balloting also provides an efficient way to assess where participants stand. Without it, group members waste time trying to convince each other about their line of thinking. Participants don't need to agree on the same reasons in order to agree on the same result.

The reality is that people don't think about issues in the same way. Most businesses and organizations, even tightly knit ones, have an array of interests and perspectives, analogous to an elephant, which looks different, depending on whether you are viewing it from the front, back, side, or top. People at each perspective tend to argue that their view is correct, but when they step back from their personal vantage points, they can all agree that what they're looking at is an elephant. Similarly, secret ballots enable groups to cut through differences in perspective and uncover common ground.

Despite its benefits, some people resist secret balloting because they fear the intrusion of power politics and the possibility of a majority overriding the legitimate concerns of a minority. This is not, however, an inherent problem of secret balloting; rather, it is an issue of how you use the balloting results. Step #8 provides a constructive way to discuss these results.

Secret balloting is cheap, fast, and effective; it stimulates thinking, exploring, and writing; and it provides an action-oriented way to draw the ten-step process toward a conclusion. Unfortunately, very few organizations take advantage of this powerful tool. More than 40 percent of the dozens of organizations surveyed had never used an approach like this (see Appendix A)—they simply guess about where their stakeholders actually stand on a given issue. But with some paper, pens, and a few minutes' time, they can take the guesswork out of their decision making and thereby enable their teams to be more productive and successful.

PUTTING STEP #7 INTO PRACTICE

1. *Confirm in writing the final options for consideration.* Designate each option with a letter, in alphabetical sequence, for easy

reference. Then survey the group to see whether anyone would like clarification of any of the options. Resolve any uncertainties or differences in understanding about the choices being considered.

2. *Review your shared hopes.* The hopes you outlined and shared in Step #2 will help you align for action. Review these hopes before you begin to express preferences. Ask each participant in turn to read one hope aloud in sequence.

3. *Allow a few minutes of silence for each person to reflect on the options and how they relate to the group's hopes.* Give everyone time to let their thoughts settle and relinquish their inclination to control the outcome. Think about what you've heard from the other participants. Stay open to any new perspectives that emerge and allow your inner wisdom to guide you.

4. *Ask each person to write down the option that best fulfills the hopes the group shares and to draw a circle around that choice.* Encourage participants to focus on the group's shared hopes, not on individual agendas. The former will serve the greater good.

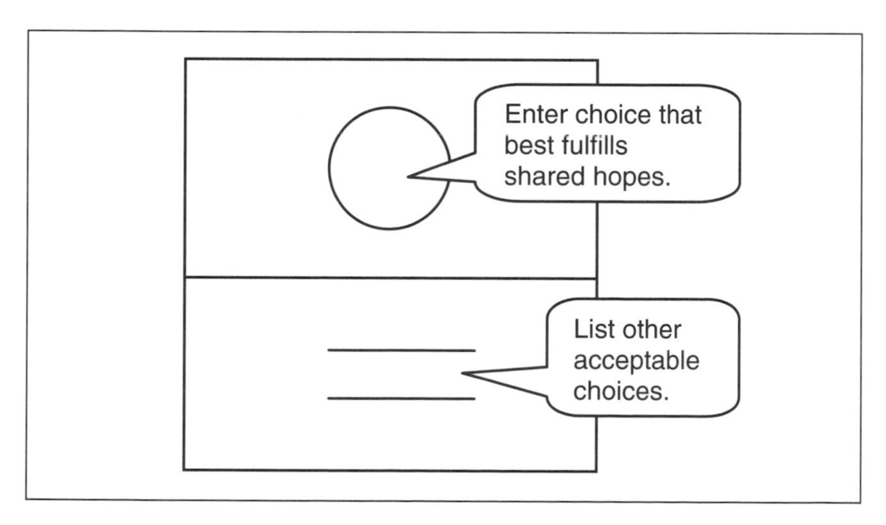

FIGURE 12 Use secret ballots to capture each person's best thinking.

5. *Below the circled choice, list any other options that would be acceptable and help fulfill your aims, albeit not as effectively as the first choice.* Include any options that would be acceptable ways to advance your hopes so that there are alternatives in case the first choice proves unworkable. (See Figure 12.)

6. *Use secret ballots.* Fold the slips of paper on which group members have written their choices and submit them for tabulation. Now you're ready for Step #8, in which you'll map the solution spectrum and discover the results that are best for your group.

BE AN AGENT OF HOPE

Each person is a powerful instrument for discerning desirable courses of action. When participants tune their instruments to the hopes they share, they produce valuable wisdom. The secret ballots record the information so that you can gain the full benefit of this wisdom.

STEP #8

Map the Solutions

See Clear Results

Things seen are mightier than things heard.
—Alfred, Lord Tennyson

Once the secret ballots have been cast, it takes just a moment to tally the straw vote. Once you have the tally, you'll quickly discover exactly what each participant thinks is the best choice, as well as potential alternatives.

Let the results from the secret ballots speak—and speak quickly—for themselves. Steps #1 through #7 provided extensive opportunities for sharing information. Now is the time to look at the results and let participants learn from them.

STEP #8 IN ACTION

Tough Issue: *Reaching Agreement on Future Products*

Tim's R&D team members, who were trying to determine the best path to their next generation of products (see the example in Step #6), braced themselves for the results of their secret ballots. They had already identified three possible solutions and, following Step #7, had cast their secret ballots. As they waited for the ballot results, many questions swirled around: "Which approach do you think garnered the most support?" "Were the last two hours of discussion worth it?" "Will there be a clear agreement that fulfills our hopes for a shared platform to develop new products, or will we be back where we started, with no agreement and no path for moving forward?"

A Great Decision Solution

The ten-member group had cast their votes for option A, B, or C, circling the best choice for the group and adding any other viable alternatives. Option A was the status quo approach of multiple, incompatible software systems. B and C represented different choices for a common software development system.

Now, they tallied the ballots on a large piece of flip-chart paper for everyone to see. One of the group members recorded the ballot results and completed the Solution Finder chart as shown in Figure 13. She entered a tick mark in the row on the left-hand column that corresponded to the option listed as the first choice on a ballot. Then, she added tick marks along that row in the columns corresponding to the other choices the ballot listed as acceptable alternatives.

As you can see in Figure 13, the majority of the group thought B was the most desirable option for pursuing the group's shared hopes. It received seven first-choice votes and two votes from members who thought C was the best solution but that B was an acceptable alternative. Option C trailed with a total of three first-choice votes and five persons who considered it a viable alternative to B. As much as everyone had previously resisted deciding upon a common software system, no one included that status quo option (A) on a ballot. Thus, the group focused on option B and discussed opportunities to incorporate elements of option C. They decided on B as their first choice, with C as a backup.

Through working together, participants in this process found agreement together. They overcame their fears—even their fears

1st Choice	(acceptable alternative) A	(acceptable alternative) B	(acceptable alternative) C
A			
B ✔✔✔✔✔✔✔	✔✔✔		✔✔✔✔✔
C ✔✔✔	✔	✔✔	

FIGURE 13 Example: Solution Finder reveals best choices.

that they would never find a solution upon which they could agree.

THE KEYS TO STEP #8

View Potential Solutions to Find True Agreement

Using the Solution Finder chart and letting everyone immediately see the results will provide you with an accurate basis for determining the desirable courses of action on a given issue. In more than 90 percent of the cases—even those in which stakeholders had previously battled in court—groups come to an agreement that everyone can support. Why? Because they follow a process that enables them to discover their shared hopes and openly explore desirable opportunities to pursue those hopes together.

In the rare instances where significant differences remain, you may need to discuss the alternatives further and come up with some fresh options. Then you can return to Step #6 to evaluate them and continue with the process to find the best solution and a shared commitment for implementation.

Display Results Visually to Reduce Ego Obstacles

With ballot results displayed before them, participants readily gravitate to the options that have potential. People who are stuck on their original idea may discover that it lacks support.

For example, on Tim's software team, the one person whose ballot didn't include B as either a first choice or a viable alternative accepted the group's decision after seeing the results. Because the process was open and no one dominated the discussions, this group member didn't lose face by expressing a different choice. But the decision process, and the displayed results, enabled him to see the picture from other participants' perspectives and, in the end, he willingly supported the team's choice.

Use the Solution Finder Chart to Clarify Alternative Choices

Using Step #8 and the Solution Finder chart not only highlights the preferred option, but also makes the viable alternatives readily apparent. That's why it's important to include both a preferred choice and acceptable alternatives on the ballots and display all the results. Because the alternatives are also tallied, the group is able to explore them further and perhaps incorporate some of their strong points into the chosen solution.

Explore Ways to Improve the Most Attractive Options

Step #8 provides you with clear results and avoids the divisiveness and long-winded debate that can accompany other decision-making approaches. Another advantage is that it lets you incorporate features from alternatives that received significant support. For example, after tallying the votes, the software group discussed what was especially appealing about option C to the participants who selected it as the best choice. Although the group agreed to pursue first-choice B as their new design platform, they modified it to include some compatible elements from option C. Thus, the ballot results provided a way for discussing the options and improving the chosen solution, rather than a means of forcing the majority's view on the minority. And they completed the whole process during the course of an afternoon meeting.

You'll note that this process does not require consensus. That is, it doesn't insist that everyone agree that a particular choice is best in order to proceed. Consensus is desirable if it occurs honestly, without pressure that everyone conform to the same thinking, and if it produces high-quality results. Unfortunately, consensus-driven decisions often fall far short of this ideal. Participants may opt for the least objectionable decision or the lowest common denominator of their interests. Some participants will inevitably mask their honest assessments in an effort to find a compromise with others.

In contrast, the ten-step process encourages all participants to express their candid views and find a shared solution. This brings inventive ideas to the surface. Since it refocuses attention from personal wins and losses to shared results, participants agree upon and support the final decision even if it wasn't the choice they personally preferred.

PUTTING STEP #8 INTO PRACTICE

1. *Tabulate the secret ballots on the Solution Finder chart.* For each ballot, mark one tick in the first-choice column for the option circled on the ballot. Follow the row over from the first choice and put tick marks in the columns for the other acceptable alternatives on the ballot. (See Figure 14.)

Solution Finder

1st Choice	(acceptable alternative) A	(acceptable alternative) B	(acceptable alternative) C	(acceptable alternative) D
A				
B				
C				
D				

FIGURE 14 Use a chart like this to tabulate results and find solutions.

2. *Look for the best solution.* When you look at the results, determine whether there is a clear first choice. Frequently, most, if not all, participants list the same option. If that's not the case, check whether the sum of the first-choice votes for an option and the listings of the option as an acceptable alternative include votes from all the participants. Such a choice would likely be a good solution.

3. *Explore the possibility of incorporating attributes from other favored solutions.* Examine closely the other options that received first-choice votes. What features do they offer that might be incorporated in the desired solution?

4. *Identify an alternative solution.* Which other option has broad support? Take time to develop this alternative to the point that the participants would support its implementation if the preferred solution became less desirable.

5. *Confirm the preferred solution and the alternative solution with all participants.* Although some participants may not have listed the solutions that the group chose as their first choice, or even as an acceptable choice, determine whether they can support the decisions reached as the legitimate result of a process they followed together.

BE AN AGENT OF HOPE

A picture is worth a thousand words. Use the Solution Finder to let the results speak for themselves and guide participants to select and improve upon desirable choices.

STEP #9

Look Ahead

Be Prepared with Alternatives

Constant change is here to stay.
—Anonymous

Effective solutions to tough problems often require midcourse corrections. If the final solution were clear, the issue wouldn't have been a tough one to begin with. So don't be surprised if you start implementing your solution and find that change becomes necessary. In fact, prepare for it.

If you have followed the previous step completely, you will have one or more acceptable alternatives to your first-choice pick. Choice gives you power—the power to follow your hopes, learn from change, and adapt successfully.

People naturally want their chosen solution to succeed. They've worked hard to come to agreement on it and they have a stake in making sure it resolves the issue. But when there's only one agreed-upon solution, it can be difficult to recognize that it's not working. Denial sets in. Participants may disregard or downplay contrary information. Furthermore, those who do perceive shortcomings as a solution unfolds may hold back from telling others for fear of appearing disloyal.

Change is frightening unless you have a backup solution. So, no matter what your feelings are, stick with the process and arm yourself with one or more alternatives. Then, monitor how your data and experience fit not only with the solution you've chosen but also with the acceptable alternatives. If you pack a reserve along with your main parachute, you'll take bigger leaps with less fear.

STEP #9 IN ACTION

Tough Issue: *The Software Solution Needs Modification*

The R&D team members that reached agreement on option B in Step #8 thought their choice would work for months, maybe even years. Yet only two weeks after picking it as the best platform for new-product development, they discovered a hitch. "We can't get the software to work effectively with one of our revolutionary designs to make computers easier to use," reported a team member. "Without this application, we won't have the common platform and breakthrough applications we hoped to achieve."

A Great Decision Solution

Road bumps like the one the R&D team experienced occur frequently. In fact, the need for change arises several times faster than people anticipate. Technologies evolve rapidly. Markets fluctuate with new regulations or new players. Consumer preferences and competitive dynamics shift at a blistering pace. Many businesses struggle to keep up, recognizing that they are missing key opportunities because they don't change quickly enough. Similarly, communities flail away at making decisions about critical improvements in education, transportation, and other infrastructure requirements long after the needs first arise. Many groups find that the square peg no longer fits in the square hole. The square hole has become round or closed altogether, and is now surrounded by new holes that have opened up elsewhere.

It's natural to want more stability than is possible. Teams often discover that new issues arise as they apply their solutions to the original problem and learn how they work. However, teams can bounce back from the problems brought on by rapid change. The R&D team in this example quickly recovered from its setback and succeeded in addressing its problem because it had another available solution. Option C, which the members had approved as an acceptable alternative, worked effectively with the new application and thus became the chosen path. Since the group had taken part in an open process without the drawbacks of personal advocacy, this shift to an alternate option occurred without bruising any egos or causing divisive battles. Although the initial solution didn't work, the overall process did. The team succeeded in its important quest to build on each other's work and create breakthrough product opportunities.

THE KEYS TO STEP #9

Be Fearless in the Face of Change

Why do typical decision processes fall short of their mark? A prime factor is participants who try to prove their own individual points of view. They lock their groups into an us-versus-them dynamic. The "victors" glory in their success, which is often short-lived. The "losers" look for ways to prove themselves right and frustrate implementation of the solution. After battling to a final decision, no one has the energy to revisit the decision anytime soon. Participants often feel that too much has already been invested; thus, they become stuck in outdated decisions.

In our conflict-ridden culture, where opponents pit themselves against one another, people deride leaders who change their minds. But changing direction is not necessarily bad. Most criticism arises as the consequence of people overselling previously held points of view. In their zeal to "win" or demonstrate that they had the best idea, they refuse to acknowledge alternatives or recognize events that warrant change. Using Step #9 in particular and the entire ten-step process in general protects you from becoming victim to these debilitating dynamics.

Keep the Learning Cycle Working

Think of decision making as an ongoing process rather than as a specific end result. As Part 1 pointed out, you can visualize decision making as a continuous learning loop. The loop begins with the awareness of change and proceeds through the consideration of options, the selection of a desirable direction and viable alternatives, and then implementation of a chosen solution. It concludes with monitoring and modifying the chosen direction as new changes occur. Successful organizations move continuously through the learning loop. (See Figure 15.)

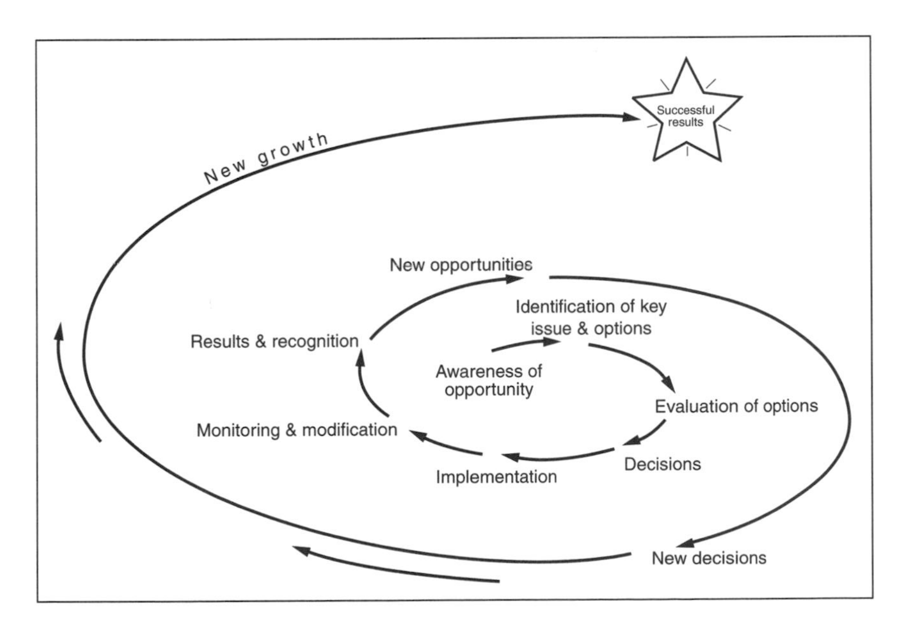

FIGURE 15 Continue the learning cycle to succeed.

Where is your organization stuck? What changes have occurred with which your decisions and solutions haven't kept pace? Are people denying change or avoiding it because they don't have viable alternatives? Maybe you have a product that isn't selling well, an inefficient production system, or team members who aren't playing effectively off each other's strengths. Wherever your problems are occurring, the ten-step process, and Step #9 in particular, will pull your group out of its rut.

PUTTING STEP #9 INTO PRACTICE

1. *Be prepared to change direction.* Identify a preferred direction as well as viable alternatives. Participants must remain alert to the key indicators about how the selected direction is working. Consider whether the acceptable alternatives have become more desirable as solutions to the problem at hand.

2. *Encourage active inquiry into the efficacy of your decisions.* Avoid communications that discourage openness. Saying "Let me know if you have any problems as you implement the decision" conveys the impression that the decision is the implementer's problem to work out. The implicit message is "Don't bother me. If this option doesn't work, you handle it." As a result, groups may fail to address change in a timely way and make accusations rather than corrections. Instead, emphasize that everyone on the team has a role in monitoring the results. Reaching agreement together is only one phase in the journey to outstanding results.

3. *Model positive inquisitiveness for your organization.* Ask: "What have we learned about the choice we made? Are any of the alternatives starting to look better?"

4. *Estimate the expected life of your decision and review your choice no later than halfway through it.* Estimate the length of time

during which you think your decision will be valid, then cut that time in half. Conduct a thorough review at that halfway point.

5. *Regard changing your mind as a positive attribute.* In fact, welcome change. Monitor and modify your decisions to incorporate it. Include change as an important part of your organization's learning loop.

BE AN AGENT OF HOPE

Embrace change with a viable set of alternatives. Choices encourage participants to perceive and respond to change more quickly and successfully.

STEP #10

Stay Charged Up

Celebrate Results and Renew Your Hopes

Nothing great was ever achieved
without enthusiasm.
—Ralph Waldo Emerson

Whether you are a top executive, a middle manager, or a team member, you have tremendous potential as an agent of hope. You can use the simple, often subtle actions of the ten-step process to help your group shift from fear-filled dynamics to hope-filled results.

Unfortunately, typical recognition systems in business, education, and many other areas focus on individual achievement and competitive results, not cooperative success. Many people get hooked on stories about conflict (who did what to whom) or winners and losers rather than on examples of how people worked together. Managers ask for teamwork, but they reward individual achievement. This is fear at work: fear that you won't stand out, that someone will advance at your expense, that you're not in charge, or that you don't deserve to be in charge.

Even informal measures send strong signals about what's valued. For example, some organizations have more parties for people who are leaving than they have to celebrate effective results among those who stay. Think of the message that a pattern like this conveys. It's probably not the one you want.

If you want your team to be its best, you must reinforce the members for pursuing their shared hopes rather than their personal agendas. This sounds good, but it is easier said than done. Praise for contributing to a successful multiperson team feels much more diluted than the glory of being the "most valuable player." Thus, team effort merits extra recognition.

This step shifts the typical dynamics and constitutes the important conclusion to the process. It's the resource that will keep your hopes energized and your process of learning, growing, and succeeding flourishing.

STEP #10 IN ACTION

Tough Issue: *How to Recognize Successful Results*

How could Tim's R&D team, described in previous steps, sustain its constructive work? Although they reached a breakthrough decision on their next generation of products, what would happen on future highly charged issues? Would the group stick together and follow the constructive process or fall back into the bickering that had them disagreeing about even the mundane details of their office furniture?

A Great Decision Solution

Recognition for the R&D team came in the form of a party. It hadn't been long—just a couple of weeks—since the team members had been wrangling over the color of the couch for their company lounge. But having carried out the first nine steps of the ten steps in this process, they had managed to agree on the path to follow together toward the next generation of products that would be important to the continued success of their company.

Step #10 was the last, but far from the least important, step for them to put into practice. During an afternoon party held in honor of their cooperative achievement, the team members relaxed, enjoyed some refreshments, and offered their impressions about how their decision supported their shared hopes: "We chose a solution that will support each of our innovations," one person said. Another chimed in, "I'm excited and want to get rolling. This gives us a reason to work together." Someone else commented, "The result wasn't my first choice, but I see how it's the right one for our business." The team members had created a new story for themselves and reinforced the process by celebrating their work and the decision they made by working together.

Tough Issue: *How to Sustain Progress and Fulfill Your Hopes*

How could the operations and maintenance groups at the industrial plant described in Step #4 sustain the positive progress they gained in solving the million-dollar-a-day turbine problem together? They had a legacy of decades of conflict. How could they avoid falling into those old patterns when new problems arose?

A Great Decision Solution

The operations and maintenance team took Step #10 to another level. They not only celebrated their immediate results but also agreed to formally review their progress toward fulfilling their shared hopes on a periodic basis. Both departments joined the plant manager for a special luncheon six months later. They talked about how they carried the process forward, what they learned from their projects, and how much progress they made toward their hopes of becoming a team and being a benchmark plant.

Each person completed an anonymous survey about their progress for each of their thirteen shared hopes. They celebrated the results, which showed achievement of over 70 percent of their long-term hopes. When asked about the prospects for sustaining and fulfilling their hopes in a highly competitive industry, they reported confidence that they would fully achieve 90 percent of their ambitious list of hopes. In a matter of months, they overcame decades of strife, gained important results, and aligned themselves for a successful future.

Celebrations don't have to be time-comsuming or costly. But it is important that you offer some form of recognition to reward the effort and support continued pursuit of your hopes for the future.

THE KEYS TO STEP #10

Offer Extra Recognition for Successfully Uniting Around Your Shared Hopes

Overcoming a culture built on fear-based messages and incentives demands commitment and a plan. It requires a shift from scoring points off of each other to earning points together. But this transition won't just happen on its own nor will it happen based solely on your own will and actions. The larger story calls for you to let go of your personal agenda to allow something bigger and better to happen.

To some degree, this is a leap of faith. As you've read in the examples throughout this book, however, there is a proven path that you can follow. When the members of a group embark on this path together, they are able to create their own new story. And when that happens, a celebration is in order. The reward not only recognizes their thoughtful and effective work, but also encourages everyone to continue it.

Share Your Story with Others

If you have successfully completed the first nine steps in the process, you have rewritten your group's story. Congratulations! You've made the transition from addressing tough issues by means of a battle of fears to doing so through a dialogue of shared hopes, from fomenting a clash of egos to coming together as a team, from fueling divisiveness to establishing a healthy decision-making process that yields enduring results.

When you do something so important, you need to share your story with others and retell it for yourselves. Describe the process by which you included all concerned parties and found constructive ways to discover your shared hopes and uncover the real issue you needed to address. Note how you got many options on the table and identified their strengths and weaknesses without divisive debate. Highlight the new options you developed that no one had offered before. Acknowledge that all participants provided their candid assessments of the best solution option as well as acceptable alternatives. Affirm your satisfaction that this process yielded widespread agreement and that even the diehards supported it.

The core values of an organization reside in the stories that its people tell about it. Be sure that your story reflects the hopes you share not only for the decision-making results you aim for but also for the way in which you work together to achieve them.

When you tell your new story to others, choose your phrasing carefully. As neurolinguistic research tells us, the words we use affect our patterns of thought. Consequently, it's important to speak of your "hopes" rather than your "hurdles," and "opportunities" rather than "obstacles." This isn't an attempt to sugarcoat reality. Rather, it's an intentional effort to reframe the way you and your team think about your work and relationships. It's a way to equip yourselves to overcome the pervasive forces of fear that block the achievement of creative and constructive results.

Just as you have a choice of whether to succumb to your fears or soar with your hopes, you have a choice about the story you tell and how you tell it. You can rely on the tabloid version about who did what to whom, or you can share the good news about your team working together at its best.

If you and your group are in the public eye, be sure that you share your story with the media. Otherwise, reporters are apt to follow their typical pattern of highlighting controversy and conflict. They need to know that you are pursuing an inclusive, collaborative path and acknowledge the hopes you share in this effort. They also need to be informed when you successfully reach your goal.

When the industrial plant shifted from its unilateral development plan to a collaborative plan with extensive community involvement (see the example in Step #1), the company spread the news through public officials. Media editorials endorsed both the process and the result. Similarly, when a city council with a history of rancorous debate and divisiveness used the ten-step process and reached agreement on budget goals, the mayor highlighted the council's ability to work together on behalf of residents in his remarks to the press. The local newspaper editorial bestowed bouquets instead of brickbats on the council.

When you share your new stories, you include everyone in the celebration and enable the successful learning process to continue.

Use Celebration to Fuel Sustained Results

Celebrations provide the ritual and remembrance that secure stories in our consciousness. Lavish events are not required. Even on a shoestring budget or with no budget at all, you can recognize your shared hopes with your team and reinforce the constructive results you've achieved through them. How does your ultimate decision honor the hopes you have shared? What new ideas arose from the discussions your group conducted throughout the ten-step process? What did you learn about the issues that are important to your group members that you want to keep in mind for the future? How did it feel to reach an agreement in this way? Reviewing your successes in this way can be a constructive activity that will help to sustain team members' motivation.

After the committee on school overcrowding, mentioned previously, reached its conclusions, every committee member supported the final report to the community that detailed the recommended course of action and possible alternatives. The committee members shared their amazement at this. An elected official mused, "This is the first time in decades that the diverse factions of our community have come to agreement on anything." Another committee member observed, "When we talked at the start about our hopes of both solving the school overcrowding issue and rebuilding the fabric of our community, I was skeptical. I thought that if we could just reach an agreement to solve the overcrowding, it would be a big success. But we accomplished much more. We really have set this community and its many diverse interests on a new track of working together."

By discussing and celebrating their work and the great results they achieved, committee members realized what they had accomplished and felt confident that they could continue to produce outstanding outcomes.

PUTTING STEP #10 INTO PRACTICE

1. *Take time to recognize how the team's decision supports the hopes you share.* Invite participants to take a few moments at the end of a session to describe their experiences and how their work together contributed to the hopes they share.

2. *Tie activities and results to the team's shared hopes and values.* Show participants how actions link with your aspirations as a group. For example, when a large service business developed a series of improvement projects, the organizing team described each project and listed the specific hopes and values it supported. At a celebration of project results, presenters underscored these motivating values. They explained what they had hoped to accomplish, how they had worked together, and the results they had realized.

3. *Keep the story focused on "us," not "me."* It's so easy to step into the limelight as individuals rather than going forward together. This is especially true when you are subject to media scrutiny. To prevent this from happening, and to maintain the focus on group results, work to keep participants from becoming committed to a particular point of view during the process, before the group completes its task. For example, the committee on

school overcrowding shared information, interests, and concerns as they went along, but they did not express individual positions. This gave them the freedom to find a result all of them could support.

4. *Savor the progress.* Celebrate not only the final results but also milestones along the way. Establish periodic gatherings to review and celebrate your progress. For example, one business laid out its action plan like a treasure map. Participants identified each major milestone, and when they reached one, they took part in a specified celebration. The elaborateness of the celebrations increased from a Häagen-Dazs ice cream treat to a pizza lunch to a half day off to play paintball together when they completed the project. Find ways to mark your own progress and enjoy your exciting journey.

BE AN AGENT OF HOPE

As the saying goes, "You are what you eat." Feed on the stories of how you've worked together and pursued your shared hopes successfully. Share these with others in your organization and with the media. Give thanks for the spirit of cooperation alive in your organization. Begin a new and fulfilling chapter in the history of your group. You have the ingredients and the recipe. It's time to start cooking.

PART 3

Six Strategies for Overcoming Obstacles

STRATEGY #1

Don't Have Time? Try the 30-Minute Miracle

If you haven't had the time you think you need to solve tough issues with your team, take a deep breath and exhale. Even if you're gripped by fear and you and your group are in the critical red zone, there is a way back into the black. In just thirty minutes (large groups may need a bit more time), you can take hold of just about any issue and produce the creative results you seek.

You must use the thirty minutes wisely, however. Fast action can create a lot of heat but little light. Unfocused speed can distract you from the real issue to the consequences of not getting the issue resolved. This, in turn, triggers fear, which steals time from dealing with the real issue and stands in the way of achieving great results.

"Decision making around here is like a pinball game," complained Lynne, the sales and marketing manager for a start-up company's new graphics product. "We bounce from one decision to another. Our company managers pride themselves on how fast they decide issues. Unfortunately, our team doesn't take the time to sort through what's really happening and how we can thoughtfully respond. So, our quick decisions lead to many hours wasted on false starts, dead ends, and painful regrouping."

When time is short, a speedy way to real results is to concentrate on what you truly want to accomplish, then reframe the issue, and discover new options. You can work miracles in a small amount of time by staying focused on your hopes and taking fast but focused action.

ONE HALF HOUR, ONE WHOLE SOLUTION

The first thing you need to do is take a realistic—and honest—look at the time limitations you face. You can always find half an hour, and that's all you need to employ this streamlined, fast-forward technique for identifying options or choosing among them. (For an issue with many ramifications, you'll need additional time to employ the full technique.)

If you're starting from scratch, you'll use your half hour on Steps #1 through #4 to develop a powerful set of solutions. If you've already identified your options and gathered all the relevant information (which includes Step #5), you'll use your time on Steps #6 through #10 to bring your final choices to closure for implementation.

Thirty Minutes to Identifying Great Solutions

Lynne, the sales and marketing manager, used the quick-start version of Steps #1 through #4 to get the results she needed on a pressing marketing issue. One month into the quarter, sales of her newly launched graphics product lagged behind projections. She knew she had to boost sales fast. The deadline for placing an ad in a key publication was only two days away, and she was sweating under the pressure of deciding which ad to run.

Instead of letting the deadline drive her, Lynne took another tack. She asked herself if she was worrying about the time she had to make the decision or the time she needed to get long-term results. She reminded herself that her team had two months to boost quarterly sales, which was a lot longer than two days to decide about the next month's ad. With this realistic assessment, she was able to breathe a little easier, shift mental gears, and allow herself thirty minutes to better understand her team's choices.

Here's what she did.

Step #1: Enlist Everyone

Lynne asked the key people who understood the issue to come to a meeting. She invited the full team responsible for the new product and its sales, including product designers and sales and marketing people. She also e-mailed the field sales force, requesting input from distributors and prospective customers. "I know we're all jammed for time," she wrote, "but let's give ourselves a half hour tomorrow morning to get a grip on what's happening and how to respond."

Step #2: Discover Shared Hopes

Lynne asked all those present at the meeting to express their hopes in order to focus on the real objectives. Each of the seven attendees took about a minute to voice his or her hopes for the product and its sales. No one wasted time repeating ideas.

While the quarterly sales goal loomed before them, the team's hopes took a broader form. For example, the field sales representative said, "I hope we attract some quality customers who will create 'buzz' and word-of-mouth referrals that will help us draw more customers." Fulfilling this hope would build sales and sustainable profits. This perspective shifted the group's thinking from the urgency of the ad deadline to more fundamental objectives.

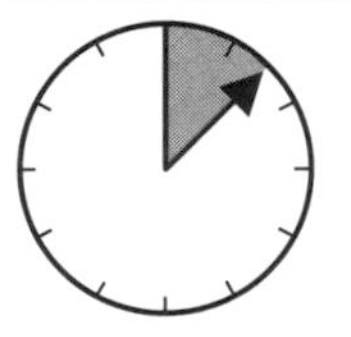

Step #3: Uncover the Real Issues

Next, Lynne invited each participant to state his or her thoughts and concerns in order to uncover the real issue. To make sure that everyone really listened, each person who spoke summarized what the previous person had said. This process of listening and reflecting, without debate or attempts to immediately solve the problem, took a couple of minutes per person.

The marketing assistant questioned the ad campaign. "Everyone is running ads," he said. "I'm concerned that more ads won't be effective with all the noise in the market. They may not attract the customers we want at this stage." Instead of defending the ad campaign, the person responsible for preparing ads reflected on what she heard. This step enabled the new perspective to sink in and helped the team refocus its efforts on different ways to build relationships with new customers.

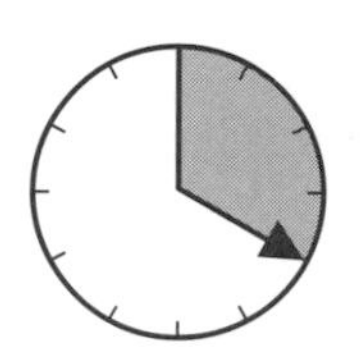

Step #4. Identify All Options

Finally, Lynne asked the group to identify an array of options for pursuing the hopes expressed. Each person stated one new option for building client relationships. In ten minutes of structured brainstorming, the group developed several promising ideas. One was to gather testimonials from satisfied customers to attract additional ideal clients. The product engineers also offered to network with their professional colleagues to build credibility for the product and stimulate buzz for positive word-of-mouth referrals. A third idea involved sending e-mails to the field to identify target accounts. The group decided to develop all of the ideas and meet later that week to follow up on implementation.

By spending two-thirds of its brief meeting time focused on fundamental objectives, the group was able to understand the real issue it faced. Deciding about an ad in two days' time turned out not to be a high priority. Instead of making a hurried decision about the ad, Lynne took time to engage key people with a broader range of perspectives and took a better look at the basic objectives, the real issue, and fresh options. By employing the thirty-minute process, Lynne and her extended team embarked on a completely new path to turn their product sales around. And the best part was that they did it together.

Choosing an Option and Moving Forward

Sometimes groups can articulate their hopes, discover the real issue they face, and put options on the table, but they just can't decide what to do from there. They may avoid deciding because they don't know how to bring the issue to closure without lengthy and divisive debate.

For example, the board of directors of a statewide professional organization wrestled for years with the thorny decision about whether to take a stand on key legislative issues. Board members talked about the problem at length, but they never resolved it. Passions ran high and members feared it would take too much time to decide. More fundamentally, they worried that they might spend a lot of time and fail to achieve agreement among the thirty-three members—or, worse, that the contentious issue might split the membership.

The board began working with the ten-step process. In previous sessions, the members articulated their hopes, pinpointed the real issue, and brainstormed a list of options (Steps #1 through #4). They also had a good grasp of the relevant information (Step #5). Now, they needed to weigh the information and make a decision.

The next time the board met, the president addressed the group. "We've got one hour," she said. "We're going to use a new, fast method to reach a decision." (Generally small groups can decide on an option in thirty minutes, but larger groups like this one may need an hour—still a remarkably short time to get more than thirty people to make an effective decision together.)

Here's what the board did.

Step #6: Get Everything on the Table

The board members began by discussing the status quo option: not taking a position on legislative issues. Each member mentioned something negative about the option and, following Step #6 guidelines, refrained from repeating or commenting on each other's statements. This saved an enormous amount of time because the board had a history of members squaring off against one another in protracted debates. After all of the negatives about the status quo were brought forward, board members followed the same process to express the positives for that option.

Next, they considered the option of taking positions on key legislative issues. They used the same process to express the potential negatives and positives. Even the most argumentative members stayed on track and expressed views on both sides of the option.

After hearing all the pros and cons on the initial options, the members came up with a new alternative: targeting advocacy on a specific set of issues. (The emergence of new, inventive possibilities typifies the successful results this step yields.)

With thirty-three participants discussing three options, this step took about forty minutes. Everyone participated. All of the relevant information got a hearing.

Step #7: Write Down Choices That Support Your Shared Hopes

On secret ballots, board members wrote their first-choice option and other acceptable options that they felt best fulfilled their shared hopes for the organization. They appreciated that they could be entirely candid by using the secret ballot. With all of the information before them, members needed only a few moments of reflection to make and write down their choices.

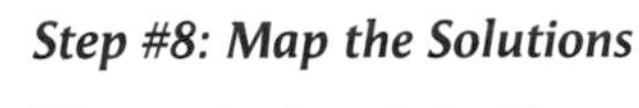

Step #8: Map the Solutions

The tabulated ballot results showed twenty-eight members favored the newly introduced option of limited advocacy. The remaining five favored no advocacy role for the organization, but they also listed the limited advocacy option as an acceptable choice for the organization. The clarity of direction pleasantly surprised the group. They spent a few minutes discussing the limited advocacy option in order to satisfy the concerns of those who would have preferred no advocacy.

The tabulation and follow-up discussion took only ten minutes.

Step #9: Look Ahead

After the decision, the board assigned a small group to develop the details of the new legislative policy and a timetable for implementation. This rounded out the hour they had devoted to the issue.

Step #10: Stay Charged Up

As the president of the board commented afterward, "I'm amazed at what we accomplished. Although we had different perspectives, we agreed on a common course of action. It's a great relief to get this long-standing issue resolved."

As part of the celebration, two board members, who had been ardent adversaries in debates, tying up previous board meetings on a variety of other issues, linked arms for the group photograph at the end of the board meeting. The process not only improved the meeting dynamics but also transformed the working relationships among the board members. They accomplished something important together and had plenty of reason to celebrate.

LET MIRACLES HAPPEN FOR YOU

When you're pressed for time, take a realistic look at the issues before you and your group. Then:

- Don't let a concern about lack of time drive you to make poor decisions or avoid making decisions at all. Be honest about the actual time you have to get results as opposed to how long you think you have to decide a particular issue.
- Assess what your group needs to do. Are you confronting a fresh issue? Then you need to start with Step #1. Are the issue, its options, and pertinent information on the table already? Then you can start with Step #6 to break through the logjam

to a conclusion. (If you're faced with a fresh issue that has multiple ramifications, you'll need to take the time for the full process.)

- Let go of your fears. You have the time and resources to work together. By using the focused, quick-start process, you'll make important progress toward fulfilling your hopes.

BE AN AGENT OF HOPE

There is time to do what you really need to do. The key is discovering what that is. The ten-step process gives you the right tools.

STRATEGY #2

Not in Charge? Employ Persuasive Techniques

Many people say that they would like to institute more effective teamwork and the benefits of constructive decision making in their organizations, but they don't believe they can do anything about it. They aren't in charge and don't want to ruffle other people's feathers. These situations call for persuasive teamwork—effective ways to promote positive dynamics without triggering divisive power struggles. The people you live and work with need you to take the initiative to make this happen.

Even if you have little or no positional authority, you have the opportunity to bring the ten-step process into your workplace as well as other areas of your life. In fact, people who are not in charge often have the most freedom to take action. Here's why.

Many of the fears that arise in organizations are ego-driven. At the top levels, people want to project the image that "I'm in charge. I have the answers." They want to justify their authority. When tough issues arise, such people are at their most vulnerable. They worry that they won't know the right answer or might take the wrong path, and wonder whether others will follow their lead. When people are this fearful, their need for control soars.

People at lower levels rarely suffer from illusions about their degree of control. They have a less self-assuming posture: "I'm just here doing my job." They don't have the inflated egos that often plague people who exercise positional authority.

But even most of the high-level people—managers, elected officials, and community leaders—know that they're not completely in charge. They do think, however, that employers, voters, or neighbors expect them to have the answers and take care of the problems, and they feel trapped. Other people's expectations crowd out their hopes and initiate the self-defeating cycle of fear.

Some of the toughest situations arise when each person involved in a particular issue has positional authority, but no one has definitive control. For example, division managers from marketing and R&D need to work together to develop a new product but neither one has power to direct what the other person does. Both people have risen through the ranks as the result of their ability to get things done in the area where they are in charge, but now they can't make anything happen together. Patience wears thin, tempers soar, and tough issues fester.

In truth, control is an illusion. CEOs report to boards of directors. Boards of directors are accountable to shareholders. When it comes to dealing with the toughest issues, no one is really in total control.

Although you may not be in charge, a few simple techniques can enable you to be an agent of hope in fear-filled situations and shift the dynamics to a positive course.

THREE POWERFUL TECHNIQUES

The key theme of all three techniques is to appeal to people's better nature. Help them get out of the box of expectations that keeps them from participating in an inclusive and constructive process and stymies the possibility of achieving productive results. In addition, you must accomplish this without raising your colleagues' fears about loss of control. The following persuasive techniques will help you get better results when you're not in charge.

Technique #1: Invite People to Try a Different Approach

John's fledgling high-tech company had its back against the wall. A new software release was late. Cash was running out. Investors and creditors demanded results.

Amid these fears, John drove his management team crazy. He called meetings to discuss business issues and then dominated the discussion. This frustrated other participants, and the group failed to get to the real issues. Even John became disgruntled. "The managers won't take ownership of problems and aren't coming up with the ideas we need to solve them," he complained. In short, he suffered from his own need to control everything. His response to a mounting fear of failure was to clamp down on his company like a vise.

Fortunately, Sarah, one of the managers in the company, found a nonthreatening way to speak privately with John in advance of a meeting. She suggested that, to uncover the underlying issues, John simply identify the topic and then ask each person to share his or her thoughts about it—Step #3 in the ten-step process. John agreed that something needed to change. He followed Sarah's idea to keep the discussion moving so that no one dominated the session.

Sarah's simple initiative shifted the management team's dynamics. Team members participated more, accepted responsibility, and began to resolve key issues. "My team's starting to gel and produce results," John said excitedly. Sarah's tactful way of addressing the situation not only earned her added respect from John and the team but also created a new openness in communication that unleashed a flood of creativity. Soon, the management team had a new data storage system for a promising international market and attracted additional capital.

Control-oriented people like John generally resist someone directly challenging their authority or the way they do things. Such people are unlikely to directly adopt a new system of discussing and deciding tough issues, regardless of the process's proven effectiveness.

To sell them on the concept, you don't need to sell them on the entire process or even advocate it as a new process. Instead, you can follow Sarah's lead and take a simple action to introduce steps subtly and effectively. Sarah didn't change John's personality; she tweaked the way the team discussed issues so that the better side of John's personality emerged. This new approach halted the fear-driven cycle that had the company careening toward destruction.

Opportunities abound to do small things that make a big difference. No matter what role you play, you can improve situations. Express your invitations in ways that use the positive appeal of each step to attract interest. You may wish to outline one or two steps at a time so that the process doesn't seem too threatening or overwhelming.

To help you toward your goal, Table 4 offers everyday language and commonsense appeals that you can use to encourage others to step through the process with you. Like Sarah, you can find a tactful and convincing way to introduce the steps.

Technique #2: Offer Choices and Let Others Choose

When you encounter people who want to control decisions or actions, offer them choices. Identify two or more options that work for you and your group's objectives and then let them choose among them. For example, say, "Shall we gather the team members and other potential sources of information to discuss this topic today or at a time later this week?"

It's like offering a child who doesn't like vegetables the choice between broccoli and peas. This allows the child to control the choice, but you have the satisfaction that he or she is eating vegetables. Give people choices, and they'll more readily cooperate with you.

Technique #3: Interrupt Behavioral Patterns That Aren't Working

Workers assume that leaders and managers intentionally behave as they do. The reality is that most people in charge are not fully

TABLE 4 Inviting Ways to Encourage Use of the Ten-Step Process

PROCESS OR STEP	PERSUASIVE LANGUAGE YOU CAN USE
Overall Ten-Step Process	Let's bring everyone together to discuss this issue. We can follow a few steps that will get us through the discussion productively.
Step #1: Enlist Everyone	Whom can we involve who knows something about this issue or will need to participate in a decision about it or in its implementation? Each person is important to get real results.
Step #2: Discover Shared Hopes	Before we get started or anyone jumps to specific solutions, let's spend a few minutes to hear what each person hopes will result from the effort and why that's important.
Step #3: Uncover the Real Issues	You know, I'm not sure that the issue is really clear. It might be exactly as you've said, but let's explore it a little further. How about if we each take a few moments to express our thoughts and concerns about the topic? Before the next person speaks, let's have that person paraphrase what the previous speaker said so that we know that we've really heard it clearly.
Step #4: Identify All Options	It's good brainstorming to get lots of options out on the table before we discuss any in detail. We can go around the group and have each person offer an option that might help fulfill what we hope to accomplish. Let's not repeat anything or start agreeing or disagreeing.
Step #5: Gather the Right Information	Rather than gather information about each option on its own, we can organize our efforts by our hopes and look at all of the options from the perspective of what we really want to accomplish. That way, we will work together and efficiently collect the information we need.

TABLE 4 *Continued*

PROCESS OR STEP	PERSUASIVE LANGUAGE YOU CAN USE
Step #6: Get Everything on the Table	We could save a lot of time and debate if we went around the group and had everyone state something that might be negative about each option and afterward the potential positives. I'm sure that we could each find something to say both pro and con about each option without repeating one another. It will take us only a few minutes to hear everyone's perspectives, and we'll avoid divisive debates. We're also likely to think of even better options.
Step #7: Write Down Choices that Support Shared Hopes	Let's find out what each person candidly thinks about the choices. Each person can list what looks best to fulfill our hopes and any acceptable alternatives. This straw ballot will give us a quick look at possible solutions.
Step #8: Map Solutions	We can tabulate the results on a flip chart or piece of paper to see where all of the options sorted out. Then we can look at possible ways to improve upon the most attractive alternatives and find a solution that everyone will support.
Step #9: Look Ahead	Before we rush off to implement our solution, we need a backup plan and early opportunities to see how our solution performs and compares with acceptable alternatives.
Step #10: Stay Charged Up	People did a great job of listening to one another and searching for solutions that will serve the best interests of the group. Let's bring everyone together and hear from people about how the results support the hopes we share. It's time to celebrate what we've accomplished and encourage people to continue working together effectively.

conscious of their self-limiting behaviors. Others want to change their behavior but don't know how.

Sometimes even small changes can improve interpersonal dynamics. Try sitting in a different place, or suggest a creative teamwork game to start the meeting. Another alternative is to offer a story.

For example, I once told a story about playing tennis to a team of high-strung, overwrought executives. They wanted to perform better, and the divisive dynamics in their group frustrated them. I described how I struggled with my tennis game and pored over books with new techniques and tips—all to no avail. Then I tried *The Inner Game of Tennis* (Random House, 1974) by Tim Gallwey, who encourages developing nonjudgmental awareness of how the ball moves.

I described Gallwey's simple practice of saying "bounce" when the ball bounced and "hit" when I wanted to hit it. At first it seemed silly. Nonetheless, I continued to focus on the ball and trust that my body would perform. Soon, I outscored others who had consistently beaten me, and I did it with just a fraction of the effort I had previously expended. The exercise shifted my attention from my fears—"I'm going to miss another one! I'm going to lose this game!"—to the simple observation of how the ball moved and my intention about when to hit it.

Fears take our eyes off the ball in business as well as in tennis. We need people to remind us to stay focused on our hopes and to adhere to a process that helps us follow through.

When the management team applied the practice of nonjudgmental awareness to the way they interacted with one another, they observed each other's management style and discussed ways to honor their differences. The process shifted their behavior more quickly and effectively than further talk about management techniques would have. By changing their usual pattern, the managers found positive ways to work together.

Small, persuasive actions can yield significant results, even when you're not in charge. They also are fun. Once you start employing them as a team, you'll build your confidence that you can change almost any situation. And as long as you don't judge others and trigger their defense mechanisms, everyone will welcome your initiatives. The key to persuasive action is to introduce change without prompting participants to feel that what they've been doing is wrong. Instead of looking for an ego victory at the expense of others, use these productive techniques to make everyone a winner.

BE AN AGENT OF HOPE

Step into your power to positively change the dynamics in even the toughest situations. Introduce the ten steps cautiously, with language and an approach that doesn't threaten those who are in charge. Remember that control is an illusion. Deep down, everyone knows it.

Let the intrinsic appeal of the process work with you. When you lead with what truly are your shared hopes, you'll have the strength to guide your group forward to productive results.

STRATEGY #3

No Guide? Follow the Self-Directed Process

A moderator or facilitator can help discussions be more productive, build teamwork, and keep group members from lapsing back into old ways. But even if you don't have a specially trained facilitator (see "Choosing a Facilitator" later in this strategy for information on facilitation), you can still put the ten-step process to work right now. If your group is hemorrhaging as the result of internal conflict and no doctor is available, you can roll up your sleeves and cure it yourself. This approach may not be perfect, but it's much better than letting your hopes die.

Typical ways to decide issues and lead teams are simply falling short. As evidenced in boardroom power plays and political debates, participants fear losing ground, engage in wars of words, take cheap shots, and fail to bring people together to solve problems. The results of all this are that CEOs now typically have short tenures, elections swing on slim majorities, and people give up on their collective ability to make meaningful improvements.

The problems that arise with decision making and teamwork stem from the ways people choose to go about their work and lives together. It's a system problem, the result of a series of factors, and it requires active intervention to change it. And some people are doing just that. For example, columnist David Broder described a state political campaign several years ago that began in a fiercely negative style. The tenor of debate dramatically improved when a debate moderator insisted that the candidates speak only about their own character and ideas and not criticize those of anyone else. This format respected the observers' abilities to judge what each person presented and decide for themselves.

If no one in your organization has the needed facilitation skills, and you don't plan to hire an outside leader, you can develop the necessary skills yourself. Then you, too, can encourage a change for the better by confidently guiding your team through the ten-step process.

THE KEYS TO GUIDING THE PROCESS

The way you guide a discussion determines the quality of the results. Whether the facilitator is an outside leader, you, or someone from your group, these important pointers can help everyone produce great results.

Key #1: Establish Constructive Communication Guidelines

Positive communication guidelines include ways to respect others by speaking about issues rather than personalities. They also encourage speaking candidly and using "I" statements to take personal ownership for what is said. An effective facilitator encourages each person to participate, welcome new ideas, and listen to and reflect upon what others say.

The following list outlines communication guidelines that have proven to be effective. Before starting a meeting, post them on the wall or project them on a screen for everyone to see. Ask participants if they are willing to abide by the guidelines and whether there are any additions or modifications that would support their constructive participation.

COMMUNICATION GUIDELINES

1. Be candid—offer your best insights and ideas.
2. Speak about issues, not personalities. Use "I" statements to express your perspective.
3. Listen to and reflect on what others say.
4. Seek to find the shared wisdom within the group.
5. Be willing to let go of your position for the greater good.

Key #2: Write Down the Ten-Step Process and Keep It in View of the Group

You can refer to the "Quick Use Guide" at the end of Part 1 or write the ten steps on a flip chart. Either of these measures will help participants keep the process in mind. They can point to the steps rather than at one another when they want to bring the process back on track.

Key #3: Encourage Participants to Discuss their Hopes and Look for Common Ground

Team members need to know that they are pursuing similar objectives as well as appreciating their differences. Then they can do meaningful work together. Often, differences of opinion or divergent personal styles obscure shared interests. A facilitator helps participants plumb their hopes to find their shared objectives.

Key #4: Focus on Information Exchange Rather Than Debate

If you want a verbal wrestling match, get a referee. If you want constructive dialogue, have someone ensure that participants get their ideas out without premature judgment or debate.

Key #5: Assess Progress Along the Way

At breaks, ask participants for feedback. Are they addressing the real issues? Is participation balanced? Encourage suggestions for improvement. Participants need to retain ownership for the meeting and be aware of how it serves everyone's needs.

Key #6: Help Participants Find Shared Solutions

The most effective techniques help participants quickly see the range of potential solutions. One way to do this is to visually display a team's choices in order to depersonalize issues. Then participants can comment on the ideas without criticizing one another.

Key #7: Gain Commitment to Translate the Solutions into Results

Many good ideas go nowhere because no one translates them into action assignments. Determine what needs to be done, who needs to do it, and how and when to accomplish it.

When several people share responsibility for implementation, ask one person to "hold the bucket." This person doesn't need to do any more work than the rest, but she or he does accept responsibility for ensuring that the job gets done.

Key #8: Bring the Discussion to a Constructive Close

Ask each participant to provide a brief comment about what the group accomplished or what worked well or could have been handled better. Invite ideas about next steps. Participants appreciate the opportunity for closure. It also provides helpful feedback for future meetings.

CHOOSING A FACILITATOR

Whether you choose someone from within your team or from outside, look for these important traits:

- The facilitator should be open to new ideas, with no vested interest in a particular outcome.
- The facilitator should listen to and accurately reflect what others say.
- The facilitator should be adept at recognizing opportunities for shared solutions.
- The facilitator should be assertive in asking for personal commitment and accountability.

How do you decide whether to choose someone from within your group or from outside to facilitate the process? If you have the time and resources to reach outside your group, two key factors can help you decide which way to go:

1. The importance of the issue: Is it worth focusing on and is it worth the related expense? Tough issues usually are.
2. The trust level among group members. Often, this is the deciding factor. If participants don't trust each other, then they are unlikely to trust one of their members to guide the process. They'll worry about whether the process is actually a power play to accomplish the guide's own agenda. And it probably will be difficult for the chosen person to be both a participant and a process guide, because the person will be sorting through his or her own feelings while trying to keep the group on track with the steps.

Figure 16 displays how to choose between inside and outside facilitation resources based on an issue's importance and the level of trust within the group. When trust is high, the group often can direct itself. Nonetheless, some groups choose an outside facilitator for very important issues because they want all participants to be free to reflect and fully participate without fretting about the process. In low-trust situations, especially where an issue's level of importance or the available resources may not support an independent facilitator,

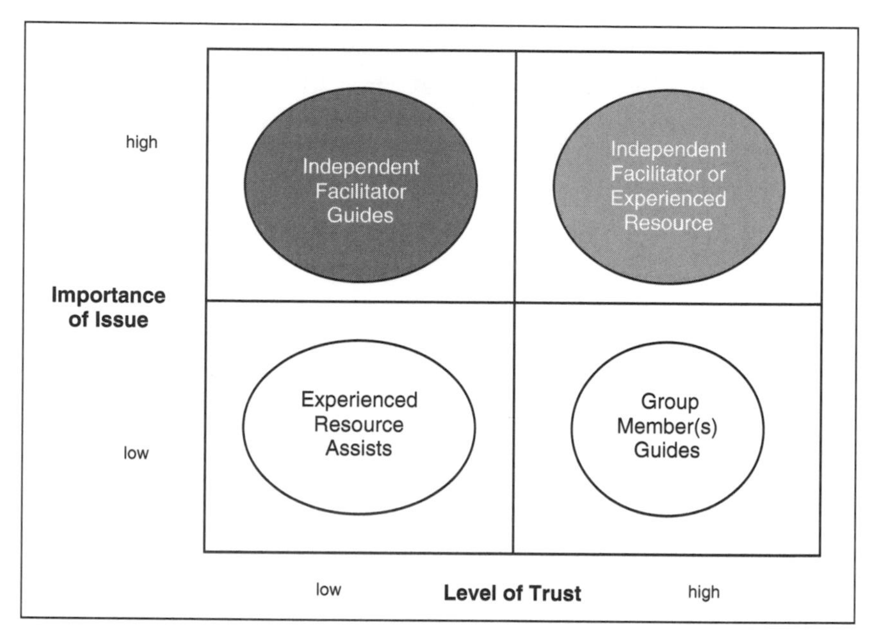

FIGURE 16 Choosing between inside or outside resources to guide the process.

you can consider tapping a person in the organization who has experience with the process to assist your group.

BUILDING FACILITATING SKILLS WITHIN YOUR ORGANIZATION: "SEE ONE, DO ONE, TEACH ONE"

Top surgeons have an amazingly simple but very powerful method for learning new procedures: "See one, do one, teach one." When a surgeon wants to learn a new procedure, he or she scrubs in with an experienced surgeon and observes the procedure firsthand. Then, the learner does the next surgery with the experienced surgeon overseeing it. Finally, the newly trained surgeon teaches the procedure to another surgeon.

This learning process is highly effective. However, many business organizations fail to employ some of its important elements. For example, a company might send someone to a seminar to learn a new skill, but the person returns without ever seeing a real application. Sometimes the person might jump into applying what was learned without the benefit of an experienced person to oversee and guide the learning process. Other learners may balk at trying because they lack confidence, abort as soon as they feel frustrated, or fumble through when unanticipated difficulties arise. Tough issues require a better level of care.

The ten-step process can provide the necessary level of care. For example, a 50-person department in a 300-employee organization used it to develop excellent "surgeons." They began as I facilitated the process to help them tackle the implementation of the computerized maintenance system that employees had resisted learning and applying for years. It was the biggest, most important issue they faced. The ten-step process enabled them to build understanding, choose an effective implementation strategy, and gain grass-roots commitment and follow-through. (See "Computer System Can't Get off the Ground" in Step #1.)

Soon, people throughout the department wanted to apply the process to their critical projects. Greg, the manager involved with implementing computerized maintenance, carried over his experience with the process to a new multi-million-dollar water development project that had been stalled among warring factions for years. I informally coached him along the way. After that experience, Greg received requests from other departments to teach them the process and serve as an in-house guide for applying it. Greg saw one, did one, and taught many others.

UNDERSTANDING THE ART AS WELL AS THE SCIENCE

The objective of this book and its many examples is to prepare you to apply the process to your own tough issues. There is a science to the process that you can learn through the steps. But there's also an art.

Years ago I learned from a Zen baker to bake handcrafted loaves of bread. He gave me the recipes that included the complex measurements, temperature readings, and timing needed to have the dough rise, form it into loaves, and let it rest before baking. I followed his instructions to the letter. I noticed, though, that my finished loaves didn't have the same crunchy crust and airy texture inside that his loaves had. "I followed your instructions exactly. I don't know what else I could have done to get better results," I lamented. "Ah," he said, "you must feel the dough and sense how it is reacting to the weather today and the fresh batch of flour we received." I had the recipe down, but I was only beginning to develop the feel.

Now that you know the recipe for the ten-step process, there are many resources to help you get the feel for using it. But whatever you do, don't wait for the perfect moment or extensive experience to start. Your business and your community need you to nourish them with a healthy way to solve tough issues.

THE RIGHT FRAME OF MIND

Your frame of mind is the most important resource you bring to facilitating the process. Facilitating meetings of talented, passionate people who are dealing with the toughest issues they face—make-or-break issues for their business or community organizations—is a gift to them and a gift for you. It's an opportunity to help people during vulnerable moments to be their better selves and find solutions to their problems together.

In doing this work, facilitators must guard against letting themselves get in the way. This doesn't mean just keeping personal biases out of the discussions of the issues. It's something deeper. Facilitators must let go of their own need to succeed so that the group can.

When I first began facilitating groups using this process, I fretted about whether the participants would come to an agreement and whether I'd look good (and have earned my fee and enhanced my reputation). I felt anxious, maybe a little defensive, and wanted to control how things went. Sounds like fear, doesn't it? How could I invite people to pursue their hopes and abandon the fear-filled dynamics endemic in their organizations when I was living in fear and projecting it in my own role?

Fortunately, Art Stevens, the spiritual guide and facilitator who taught me the spiritual traditions of this process, gave me the perspective I needed. "Facilitating this process, even doing it as a group member, is not about you. When you're at your best, you're not in charge. You've let something bigger than yourself take over."

Great, I thought, I believe that, but I forget it in the midst of the sessions. How can I make sure I remember it? Art advised, "When you start to facilitate a session, write a big '?' with a circle around it on the pad of paper you keep with you." "What's that about?" I asked. "It's a reminder to ask yourself, 'How is a greater spirit present with me and with these people at this moment in time?' " he said.

I have observed that responding to this spirit is like being in "the zone" that athletes talk about. It's trusting that we can let go of our expectations and our need to control and let something better happen. It makes the work easier and more productive.

BE AN AGENT OF HOPE

As you practice facilitating the process for your own group or others, maintain an observing, inquiring frame of mind: What deeper hopes are present among the participants? How is this situation creating an opportunity to pursue them? How shall we respond?

STRATEGY #4

Very Large Group? Solve Problems the Way You Play the Accordion

You can use the ten-step process in a wide range of group sizes and in a variety of settings: as two entrepreneurs deciding how to start their business around the kitchen table, as 50 people solving a production problem on the factory floor, or as 300 people meeting in a crowded auditorium with thousands of people watching on TV. The sky's the limit.

This strategy focuses on how to work with large groups and the simple measures you can take to scale the ten-step process to accommodate numerous people with diverse interests. Large groups offer a wellspring of energy and talent to resolve tough issues and get results, so don't be scared off. It's definitely possible to involve large numbers of people in decision making and get excellent and efficient results.

Two elements are critical:

- Having a working group serve on behalf of the large group
- Employing activities that everyone can do at the same time (parallel processing, as they say in the tech world)

MAKING DECISIONS WITH LARGE GROUPS

Many business managers assume that they can't involve everyone who has a stake in an issue or useful information to contribute. They fear that the issue at hand is too complex or that there won't be enough time to engage everyone. Other organizations are committed to broad involvement, but they bog down in reaching decisions.

Traditional decision processes that rely on one person speaking at a time break down when large numbers of people become involved. First, it takes too much time. If you wanted to hear from each of 300 people and gave each three minutes to talk, it would take fifteen hours just to get their input.

Second, public speaking isn't everyone's forte. In fact, it ranks as one of people's most dreaded activities, right up there with getting a cavity filled, firing someone, or even losing a family member. No wonder only a few people are willing to speak before large groups, and many of them show visible signs of agitation and fear.

Finally, speaking isn't the only way, or even the most effective way, of communicating and learning. Nearly equal percentages of the population prefer written communication or some active (kinesthetic) method of learning. (See the discussion in Step #4.) Thus, the public hearing approach with individual speakers bores or frustrates more than half of the participants. Is it any surprise that such large meetings fail to build understanding, bridge differences, and resolve tough issues?

The trick to working with large numbers of people is moving back and forth between all participants and a smaller group of representatives. Think of this as analogous to playing the accordion. An accordion player makes music by moving the bellows in and out while playing the keys; the in-and-out movement provides the energy. Similarly, you can move in and out among larger and smaller groups to engage everyone's ideas and energy while following the steps and resolving the tough issue that your group faces.

Resolving Issues with 50 to 300 Participants

There are three important meetings when you work with large groups in the accordion style of play. (See Figure 17.) The **A** meeting includes all participants to complete Steps #1 through #4 and legitimizes a smaller working group to go forward. The **B** meeting reviews the options and information presented by the smaller working group(s) in Steps #5 and #6 to ensure that they reflect a balanced and complete set of perspectives. The **C** meeting reviews the recommendations from the smaller working group(s) in Steps #7 through #9 and concludes with a celebration in Step #10.

Preparing for and Conducting the First Large Meeting (A)

1. Create a Base of Ownership and Involvement

Before you conduct a large meeting, assemble a few people who represent the interests in the large group to serve as an ad hoc working group. Involve them in identifying all the different interests and potential sources of information to address the topic. Employ Step #1 to get the people involved. Ascertain how you can reach them, find appropriate locations for meetings, and determine convenient meeting times. Building shared ownership with the ad hoc working group is an important factor in the success of the large meeting.

Next, invite the ad hoc working group to use Step #2 to discover the shared hopes of its members. This is the point at which participants develop a feeling for the spirit of the process. They also obtain experience at this stage, so they can guide other participants in the large meeting. They can relay their shared hopes through the announcements for the large meeting, which informs those invited to the large meeting of its purpose and goals.

Then the ad hoc working group can follow Step #3 to clarify the issue or issues that need resolution. This provides focus for the large meeting and further develops the list of stakeholders and information providers who need to participate in it.

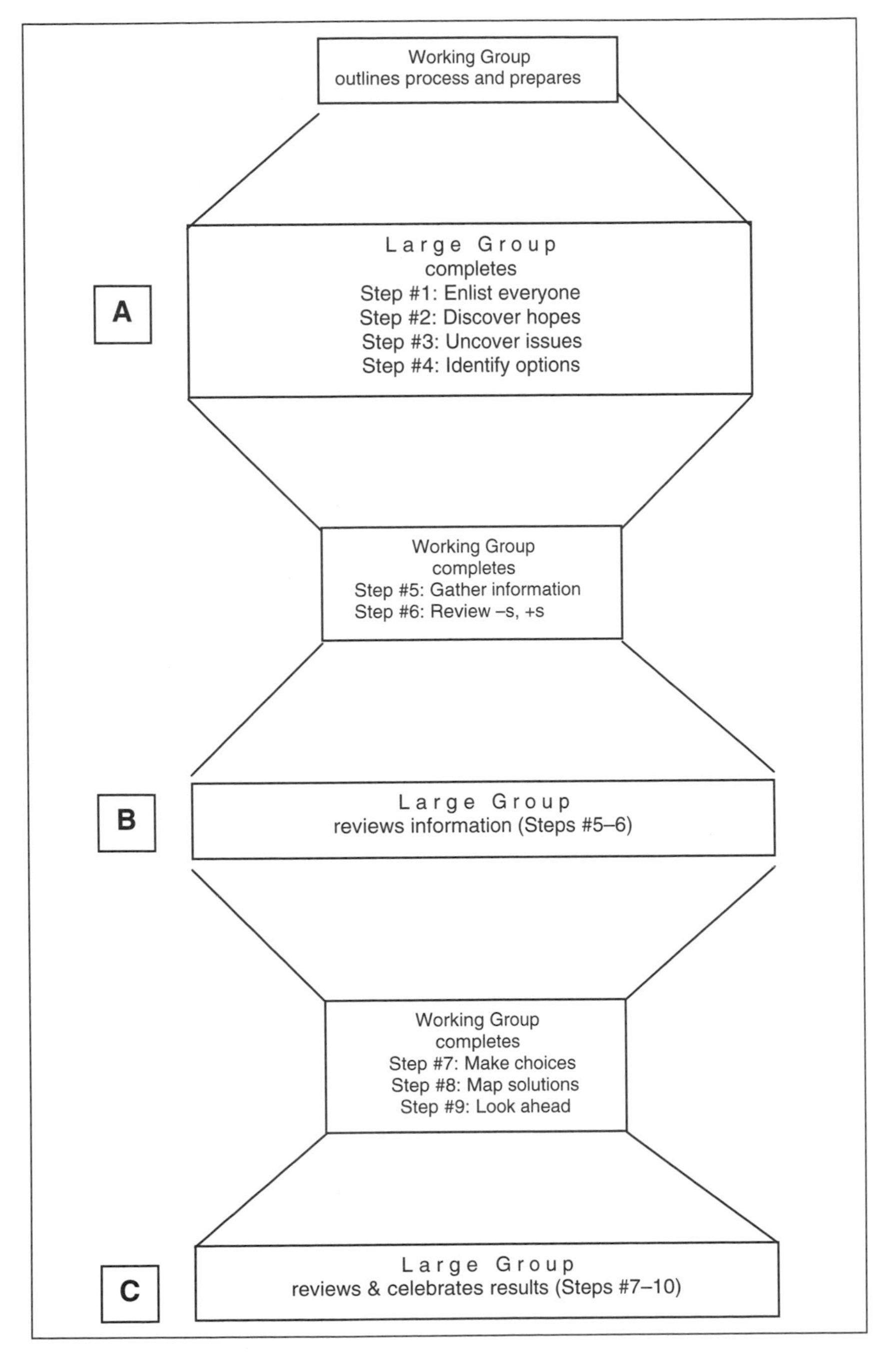

FIGURE 17 Play accordion style to work with large groups.

Finally, the ad hoc group encourages people to attend the large meeting, conveying a sincere desire for those with varying interests and relevant information to attend. The ad hoc group members distribute notices, talk with people they know, and obtain commitments from them to attend. The success of the large group meeting depends upon the diversity of interests present, not just the number of participants.

2. Add Participants and Complete Steps #1 Through #4 (Let Hopes, Issues, and Options Surface)

Bringing everyone together in the first large meeting accomplishes Step #1. At the end of the meeting, after you have discussed the issues, confirm that the relevant interests are present and identify any others that should be contacted.

Step #2 scales easily to any size group. For example, all the employees of a fifty-person engineering and construction firm wrote their hopes for the company's future on 8½- by 11-inch sheets of paper and paired off with the person they knew least well to discuss these hopes. Each partner asked the other why each particular hope was important and wrote the response on the partner's sheet. This strengthened personal connections and ensured that someone really heard what each person felt most strongly about. Participants discovered that they had more in common with each other than they had thought. When they finished, participants reported their partners' most compelling hopes. The facilitator wrote all their comments on a flip chart until they covered all of the major themes.

The meeting of 300 people to discuss the school overcrowding issue (see the "Tough Issue" described in Step #5) followed a slightly different approach. After the exchange of hopes among partners, participants posted their written hopes on a long wall. They positioned their most compelling hopes (which they starred) above the others. Then they read what others wrote and moved the pages around to cluster similar ideas together. Volunteers from the smaller working group helped to identify key themes and announced the results to the full assembly.

When this large meeting reached Step #3, participants wrote each of their issues on a sheet of 8.5- by 11-inch paper. Participants posted these on a separate wall and clustered them into themes or categories. Working group members guided participants from their prior experience with Step #3 and the categories that arose from their exercise.

Using this process, everyone aired issues or concerns efficiently and effectively. People didn't hold back out of fear of how they'd appear before the large group of people. All participants expressed their concerns at the same time without having to wait for a turn to talk. This prevented the typical meeting scenario, where a few people monopolize the group's time. Participants quickly recognized common interests and concerns without time-consuming discussion or divisive debate. A local elected official enthused, "This is the first time in years that this community has met on a tough issue without shouting matches. It makes me proud to see people working together for a change."

KEY WAYS TO SCALE STEPS #2 AND #3 FOR LARGE GROUPS

1. Ask participants to write each hope, issue, or option on a separate sheet of paper.
2. Invite them to tape their sheets of paper on a wall so that everyone sees the results.
3. Encourage them to organize the sheets of paper into common themes.
4. Summarize the results to confirm the themes.

All of these techniques adapt readily to large groups of people, and they are self-organizing. Participants do the work of clustering and reviewing the information. You can multiply the number of participants with only a modest increase in organizational resources—usually requiring a few volunteers from the ad hoc working group.

After participants identify and organize the issues, invite them to offer options for resolving the issues, either verbally or in writing, according to the Step #4 procedure. Record all the options on a flip chart. Explain that the working group will evaluate these and others as it proceeds.

3. Check the Results

Now discuss whether there are additional stakeholder interests or sources of information the working group needs to consider in order to address the issues and options identified. If there are, note these interests and then ask the group who might best represent them. Specify what interests, perspectives, or groups need representation before picking the specific people to represent them. Also confirm that you've got a complete set of issues, concerns, and options.

4. Deputize the Working Group to Proceed

At this point you need to underscore that the smaller working group's job is to serve the hopes and address the concerns of the larger group—not follow their individual agendas. This confirms and legitimizes the group to go forward on behalf of the larger group and the shared hopes of all participants.

The members of the working group serve as fact finders and option evaluators at this stage, not decision makers. In order to be credible to the larger group, each working group member must agree to set aside his or her biases and suspend advocacy of a particular position until the group completes its work together.

Preparing for and Conducting the Second Large Meeting (B)

1. Complete Steps #5 and #6 with the Working Group

The working group now finishes gathering information and noting the negatives and positives for each option. It follows the directions for Steps #5 and #6.

2. Review Information About Options with the Large Group

Share what you've learned with members of the large group. Demonstrate that the working group sought out and gathered the relevant information.

As you review the information, display the negatives and positives you've identified for each option. Confirm that all of the issues and options that members of the large group offered received consideration. Then determine whether the large group agrees with what the working group identified as the relevant negatives and positives for the options. Perhaps the larger audience knows of additional information that the working group didn't receive. Maybe there are other negatives or positives to consider for some of the options. Record this information for further consideration. Following the guidelines for Step #6, don't debate the perspectives people offer. All you need to do at this point is note the information that they provide.

If new ideas or combinations arise—which they often do when participants see everything laid out—welcome these creative ideas and identify the negatives and positives for each.

This second large meeting is critical to the credibility of the overall process. It demonstrates to all participants that working group members serve on behalf of all interests and willingly share the information they are considering before drawing conclusions.

Preparing for and Conducting the Third Large Meeting (C)

1. Complete Steps #7 Through #9 with the Working Group

After considering all the information, the working group members write down their choices (Step #7), map potential solutions (Step #8), and identify a desired course of action and acceptable alternatives (Step #9). Since the working group has tracked all of the information and done its homework, it has an in-depth level of understanding from which to make recommendations. The group members' work isn't done, however, until they bring the results back to the large group.

2. Review and Celebrate the Results with the Large Group

The way in which you communicate the results is important. Be sure to link the conclusions with the shared hopes that surfaced in the first large meeting. Describe how the working group sorted through the issues and options from the large group. Underscore the broad support for the results. Celebrate what you've accomplished (Step #10).

OVERCOMING DOUBTS AND FEARS

Most often, even highly diverse and divided groups reach a clear conclusion when they follow this process. Why? Because everyone participated. Even if each person did not participate in each step, everyone understood the process and the integrity with which the smaller group fulfilled its responsibilities on their behalf. Thus, the final decision may not be everyone's first choice, but everyone can support it.

Some people express doubts, contending that unless they participate or review the information themselves, they can't trust the results. These people are second-guessers who can erode confidence and stall results. But involving them will build their trust in the process and, in turn, their support for the results. That's why you'll benefit from a clearly defined process with periodic involvement of all interested parties.

BE AN AGENT OF HOPE

When operating with a large group, don't allow time constraints or difficult dynamics to keep you from engaging everyone who has a stake in the issue or relevant information to offer. Use the process accordion style, and move back and forth between the large group and a smaller working group. Like a good accordionist playing a rousing polka, you can get all participants to join in and enjoy themselves. As they say, "No one's unhappy when they're doing the polka."

STRATEGY #5

Can't Get Everyone Together? Be an E-Team

Whether you're working with a local group and several key people are unable to attend a meeting or you're part of a virtual team spanning time zones and cultures around the world, you can use the ten-step process to resolve tough issues. In fact, these situations particularly require the clear and inclusive method.

MEETING THE SPECIAL NEEDS OF VIRTUAL TEAMS

Global markets, fast-paced technical developments, a crunch on cash, and pressure for results have spawned virtual teams. These teams often cross geographic, cultural, and organizational lines.

For example, Chris, the president of the U.S. subsidiary of a company headquartered in Western Europe, was responsible for launching a new product in the United States. The product's lead developer worked in the Australian subsidiary. He is Scandinavian and emigrated only a few years ago. Chris needed to pull her far-flung team together to understand the technology, figure out how it might fit in the U.S. market, garner support from the parent company, and complete the product launch. But investment capital was tight, and Chris's team members needed to resolve their issues promptly and implement them efficiently. The competitive markets wouldn't give them a second chance.

If you're working with a global team like Chris's, you'll understand her dilemma. You don't have to be part of a multinational corporation, however, to have difficulties getting the right people together. Key people might be out of town. Maybe you don't have time to wait for everyone to meet, or it might be impossible to get all the stakeholders and information providers together at once. Yet you need input and commitment from everyone to be successful.

How do you resolve tough issues in a complex organizational setting? What tools can you use? Who should participate and how will they span potentially vast differences in cultures, locations, and time zones to communicate effectively?

Decision-making styles and ways of working vary. Some virtual teams limit themselves to discussing those items upon which everyone can agree. Others let dominant participants fill the leadership void. Some groups work well in person but fall apart when their members go back to their respective locations. A virtual team with outstanding talent will get caught in those dilemmas unless it finds a common process and satisfying ways for participants to plug into it.

Dispersed groups, especially those with cultural or organizational differences, particularly benefit from the ten-step process. It defines roles participants can fill and opportunities they can take advantage of wherever they are.

SELECTING THE RIGHT TOOL FOR EACH STEP

When you can't get everyone in the same place at the same time for the whole process, you can employ three simple tools to bridge the distance:

- In-person meetings (when possible)
- Video or telephone conference calls
- E-Mail

You can augment these tools with Web-based meeting tools if you want, but keep them simple. The technology needs to support the process, not distract from it.

Use the Most Personal and Direct Communication at the Start and Finish of the Process

Work through Steps #1 through #4 at an in-person meeting, if possible. You need to establish a solid foundation of mutual understanding and trust to carry forward.

If you can't meet in person, try the next best solution: a video or telephone conference call. Refer everyone to the "Quick Use Guide" located at the end of Part 1 so that they know the agenda. Also distribute any visual information or background information. Remember, too, that well-run conference calls are effective for about an hour, after which fatigue usually begins. You may need to break Steps #1 through #4 into two calls.

As you work through the process, include an opportunity for participants to meet again in person or via video or telephone conference call for Steps #9 and #10. These are important opportunities to review results and celebrate progress toward fulfillment of your shared hopes.

Use a Video or Telephone Conference Call to Evaluate Options

Step #6 requires that participants hear (if not see) one another express negatives and positives for each decision-making option under consideration. Otherwise, they won't have the assurance that each person is taking a balanced approach. In addition, the real-time exchange encourages participants' creative efforts to develop new, improved options.

Even if you are working with a large group, you can implement this step within a one-hour conference call. This time together can prevent hours of misunderstandings and delays. You can also carry out Step #8 by means of a video or telephone conference call. Send the Solution Finder chart with tabulated results to participants beforehand, and refer to the solutions mapped on it during the call.

Limit E-Mail or One-Way Web Communication to Information Exchange

Everyone has lived through some version of e-mail misunderstanding—a misguided e-mail that plagues a group or organization for weeks, months, even years. Without being able to see someone's body language or hear the person's voice, we miss the cues that provide an emotional context for a message. Was a team member's comment a criticism or just an observation? Without context, we may misread the content.

For example, a software development group struggled with a tough programming problem. A terse e-mail from its manager sent the group into a tailspin. The team members interpreted the note critically and spent hours composing and exchanging e-mail messages to defend their activities. The entire time, the manager was only a short distance down the hall. The software group finally escaped its downward spiral when members declared a cease-fire on e-mails and agreed to meet face to face to clarify the issues. The damage to productivity and relationships took weeks to repair.

Some people also fire off e-mail messages and hope that they won't have to deal with the recipients. This isn't teamwork. It's team avoidance.

E-mail isn't inherently good or bad. It's a tool, like a hammer. But it's an inappropriate tool if you keep hitting your thumb or smashing things when you need to be gluing them together.

Especially with tough issues, limit e-mails to exchanging information. Keep the messages factual and direct. In Step #5, focus on facts and perceptions without conveying any intent or appearance of advocating a particular position. For Step #7, simply submit your ballots via e-mail (or a Web tool) to someone who tabulates them.

Table 5 summarizes the suggested tools for each step, based on the specific business objectives and communication needs.

TABLE 5 Select the Right Tools for Virtual Teams

BUSINESS OBJECTIVES	COMMUNICATION NEEDS	SUGGESTED TOOLS
Steps #1–4: Form the team, discover your shared hopes, uncover the real issue(s), and identify all options.	Communication needs to be as direct and as immediate as possible—something that engages verbal and visual content as well as feelings.	a. In-person meeting b. Video or telephone conference call (with Web support and/or advance distribution of materials)
Step #5: Gather information about how the options relate to your shared hopes.	Information exchange can occur over time; immediate, face-to-face communication not required.	E-mail exchanges or Web-based posting of information
Step #6: Express negatives and positives of each option and create potential new options.	Participants need to hear that each person is providing balanced input and is brainstorming to find improved solutions.	Video or telephone conference call (with access to results via Web or e-mail distribution)
Step #7: Make choices.	Straw ballots need anonymity.	E-Mail or Web-based submission of ballots.
Step #8: Map solutions.	Everyone needs to discuss the tabulated results on the Solution Finder.	Video or telephone conference call (with access to Solution Finder results via Web or e-mail distribution)
Steps #9–10: Look ahead and stay charged up.	Participants need to confirm direction and results and celebrate how their actions link with their shared hopes.	a. In-person meeting b. Video or telephone conference call (with Web support and/or advance distribution of materials)

KEEPING THE TOOLS FROM SUPPLANTING THE PROCESS

As you work through the process, be wary of electronic tools that promise instant polling or feedback. As you work to resolve tough issues, you're trying not only to understand what people already think but also to create opportunities for them to acquire new information. The goal is to transform the issue and the participants' thoughts about it. These are the ingredients for breakthrough results in effective problem solving. This process requires personal connections and dialogue among participants, not opinion polls.

Improvements in technology will certainly make communication more interactive. As you consider the new developments, however, review the objectives and requirements for each step to assess how new tools will serve them. And remember that, although innovative communication hardware is appealing, effective human software needs to drive its use.

BE AN AGENT OF HOPE

Virtual teams offer great opportunities to tap the best talent. They also require special attention to combine the talent successfully to resolve tough issues. A clear process and thoughtful selection of tools will guide you through this minefield to realize your objectives. Take the initiative to tap these resources effectively.

STRATEGY #6

Stuck? Dissolve Old Differences and Build Trust

No matter how bitterly divided people may be, you can dissolve old differences and resolve tough issues together. You don't need to accept the self-limiting assumptions that people are stuck and can't or won't change. By appealing to their better side (and your own) you can build trust and move forward.

PERSISTENT PROBLEMS BREED DESPAIR

Although the Cold War is over between the United States and the former Soviet Union, cold wars continue to rage in many businesses and communities. The thinly masked anger between those with differing perspectives and interests hobbles their ability to work together.

As in the Cold War, participants in organizational battles first look for a clear advantage. Can they overwhelm their opponents? Often they can't, so they search for ways to contain the others' influence. They try to ignore opposing messages or saturate communications with their own points of view.

Persistent disagreements, personal attacks, and broken trust trap people in the cycle of fear and frustration. The ruts they're in become deeper and seemingly impossible to get out of. People who are resigned to the inevitability of intractable differences and difficulties may say things like this: "The managers of marketing and production always battle with one another." "We'll never get this new initiative past our boss. We'll have to wait until he moves to a new position or retires before we can deal with this festering issue." "We tried to resolve this issue a decade ago. After months of arguing, we couldn't reach any conclusion. I don't want to waste my time doing that again!" Or the ultimate: "We have to wait until we hit bottom, fail miserably, before this situation will change." The bottom, though, can be very deep and muddy. What if you don't hit bottom and bounce up for a long time—or ever?

Sadly, people lose confidence in each other, their organizations, and their ability to make a difference. Trust evaporates—and it will never return as long as the fight-or-flight dynamic of fear holds sway. *Trust* can be defined as the "confident reliance in the integrity, veracity, or justice of others." Debate, end runs, and power plays won't rebuild lost trust. Yet without trust, solutions to tough issues won't stick and have the resilience needed to respond to changing circumstances.

DISRUPTING NEGATIVE PATTERNS

Trust among employees or among community members builds from the realization of shared hopes. In fact, one definition of trust is "confident hope." Cultivating this kind of hope necessitates a big shift for groups that are stuck in old patterns.

Fortunately, as Part 1 highlighted, everyone has a hopeful side. It *is* possible to break out of old, damaging patterns and engage the better selves of those who participate in your decision-making group. Organizations and communities *can* discover the merits of disarmament and collaborative action when group members choose to set aside well-worn verbal weapons and shields to resolve issues and improve results for everyone.

If your organization is stuck in a rut, don't try to fix or repair the situation. Delving into who did what to whom and why the current problems arose is more likely to stimulate unproductive debate as well as deepen the rut. It will take too long to work your way out and require too much backfill. Instead, abandon your fear-driven vehicle and get a better one. Easier said than done, you may think. Participants have a lot invested in their well-staked positions; they have worked hard to get there, and they do what they think is necessary to defend them. Although it's not particularly desirable, a stalemate may feel more secure than an uncertain future.

But patterns can change. A particularly useful exercise for doing so, especially with bitterly divided business or community groups, is "Weapons and Shields." Here's how it works, using the example of Steve, a Silicon Valley executive.

Weapons and Shields

1. *Identify your personal weapons and shields.* Steve's weapons were compelling logic and artfully phrased arguments wielded to advance his interests. Trained in both business and legal skills, he had a full arsenal at his disposal. He was certifiably effective in debates on both big-picture issues and the tactics to implement them. The problem was that Steve's strengths blocked his ability to hear people who were less effective in presenting their ideas. Their "fuzzy" thoughts and feelings didn't fully compute with him. When people tried to overwhelm Steve's arguments with their emotional appeals, he shielded himself behind "proper procedures" and "correct answers." Although effective in the short term, these defensive maneuvers kept Steve from fully hearing and responding to the nonanalytical values and concerns others raised.

   Steve's weapons and shields weren't inherently bad. In many instances, his skills delivered great clarity and value in business situations, volunteer activities, and even family situations. When he stuck with them in the midst of differing perspectives and conflicts, however, they became liabilities.

What offensive and defensive measures do you take when conflicts arise? How do your natural strengths or experiences limit your ability to hear and respond to others constructively? When trying to change old patterns, examine the way you relate to others.

2. *Set aside your weapons and shields.* In this exercise, participants choose rocks to represent their personal weapons and shells for their shields. These physical symbols help each person keep his or her weapons and shields in mind. Then, everyone agrees to set them aside rather than push them so hard.

   Steve took his rocks, representing logic and verbal skills, and his shells, representing the shields of proper procedures and correct answers, and placed them outside the meeting room door. He didn't discard or bury them, because they had inherent value. He agreed, however, that for the duration of the business meeting he'd set them aside.

   When you perform this part of the exercise, be explicit about your weapons and shields. Explain their meaning to each other and give respectful feedback. Sometimes people aren't aware of the tools we employ and how others perceive them. What seems like a shield to the person who holds it may feel like a weapon to someone else.

3. *Notice the difference that disarmament makes.* Once Steve put aside his weapons and shields, he discovered that he could work with his team more effectively. He and his group came to a deeper understanding of their critical issues and found more workable solutions. Rather than feeling defenseless without his weapons and shields, Steve felt relieved that he no longer had to carry the burden of always playing the warrior role. More effective collaboration became possible, which in turn created shared responsibility for effective results.

> Steve found the Weapons and Shields exercise so powerful that he introduced it to a church organization. Its members had fought bitterly over programs, activities, and a budget shortfall to the point where some people were in retreat from the nasty rumors and endless debates. Everyone found the situation distasteful, but no one could come up with a way out of the fear-filled cycle of behavior.
>
> When the church members engaged in the Weapons and Shields exercise, one participant suggested that they place their rocks and shells on the church altar, explaining, "These are symbols of our prayerful requests for freedom from the shadow side of our talents when used against one another." The exercise set the stage for the ten-step process, which brought reconciliation for their community and growth in the number of church members and donations.

It's painful when good people become stuck in dysfunctional organizational dynamics. So if something isn't working, don't continue to grind away at each other. If your goal is to engage in more constructive encounters and reap productive results, whatever the situation, invite participants to set aside their weapons and shields. Relinquishing old patterns rejuvenates your organization and relationships.

EXPERIENCE NEW POSSIBILITIES

It's not enough just to break out of an old cycle—that merely gets people to stop digging themselves into a deeper rut. In order to move on, participants need a vision for improvement—how working together can achieve far more than they ever imagined.

In the depths of the despair and frustration with the impasse their group has reached, some stakeholders may have a difficult time even considering such hope. The process and examples presented so far in this book may not be enough for them. However, there is an exercise that may help when confronted with such a situation.

Balance Nails

Just as the Weapons and Shields exercise helps people break out of old patterns, simple games can help as well, even in the most difficult situations. Among the rain forest people of Borneo, games have a special purpose and a long history. As a tribal elder described it, "We give games to visitors when they arrive. If they play them well, we know that they visit with good intent. If they are distracted or don't play, we are wary that they've come to do mischief."

Similarly, you and your group can learn together in the games you play. One game that many business and community groups have enjoyed and found inspiring is Balance Nails, which business coach, Jeff Raim, taught me. Each participant gets ten nails to balance on the head of one nail that's driven upright into a small block of wood. The rules are simple: the nail driven into the block of wood must stay upright, all nails must balance on it at one time without any of them touching the wood block or other surface, and you can't use anything else (no glue, tape, plastic bag, or other means of holding the nails together). See Figure 18.

Most players have difficulty getting more than one nail to balance on the head of the upright nail. At best, players think they might be able to balance two or three. So how do you get all ten nails

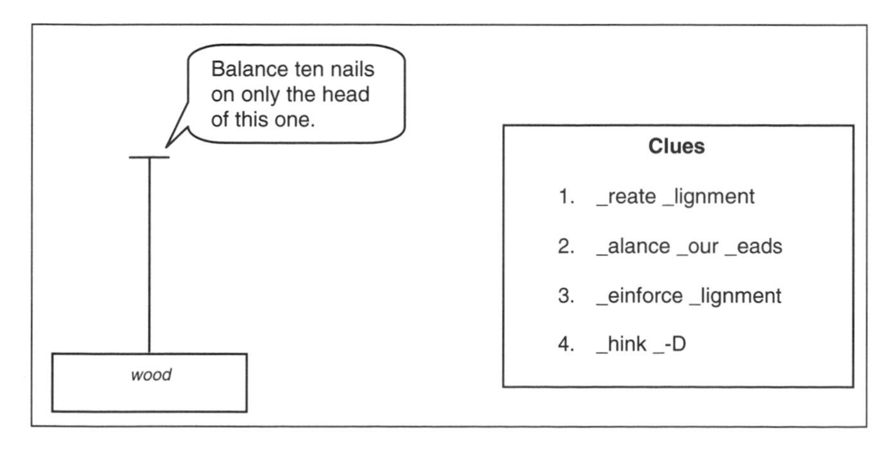

FIGURE 18 Balance Nails game.

to balance? The clues given in Figure 18, which also relate directly to the key themes of the ten-step process, will help. When you fill in the missing letters, you'll have the information you need to get all ten nails balancing on the upright nail at once. You can Find the missing letters to the clues in the footnote at the end of the chapter. If the solution eludes you, go to the Web site for this book at www.howgreatdecisionsgetmade.com. Anyone can do this—as in making great decisions together, you just need the right process.

After you've found the solution, discuss how it relates to resolving tough issues in your group. What messages does it offer about the possibilities of working together? What's similar about the solution to this game and the ten-step process? In the same way that people are surprised when they discover they can balance all ten nails, participants in the ten-step process invariably express amazement that they have accomplished something they never thought possible. They even enjoy it.

TAKE ACTION TO BUILD TRUST

Many businesses and organizations struggle because of breakdowns in trust. It's often the first issue work groups raise when they are trying to improve their effectiveness.

Recent corporate breaches of trust in energy companies, telecommunication businesses, and others, resulting in the loss of billions of dollars in market value, demonstrate the importance of trust to the bottom line. Employees, business partners, and investors want to know what information they can have faith in. If they can't trust a company's financial reports or business decisions, the company takes a huge hit.

Although much attention is directed toward devising a winning strategy or a new marketing campaign, relatively little attention gets focused on the key issue of trust. There are certain factors that erode trust and practical strategies for rebuilding it.

Missteps Erode Trust

Some of what erodes trust is intentional—dishonesty, misinformation, and greed. More often, however, actions of well-meaning people create misunderstandings. For example, an overwhelmed staff member doesn't deliver a report when promised and doesn't let others know in advance that a delay is likely. Such an erosion of trust is entirely preventable.

Similarly, misunderstandings about roles or agreements cause breakdowns of trust. People too often fail to take the few minutes necessary to summarize what they've agreed to do, why they are doing it, how they'll get it done, who else will participate, and the time frame for completion. As a result, participants tend to leave meetings with widely different understandings about what will happen. In some cases, because they haven't thought through the resources needed to complete the task and the potential impact on other priorities, what they discussed is more of a wish than a real commitment.

A failure to execute and deliver on a commitment can lead people to question other people's motives. This can start an organization down the slippery slope of distrust. As frustration mounts, threats and personal attacks often ensue.

Practical Steps Rebuild Trust

Small actions and consistent behavior restore trust. If you are unsure about whether you can support another person's point of view or request, take the time to listen and reflect back what you hear. Be sure that you understand the other person's perspective before responding. When you hear and acknowledge someone else, you lay the foundation for trust.

Be candid about your own thoughts and concerns while avoiding any personal attacks. The best strategy for this is to use only "I" statements. That is, say only what *you* observe or feel about the issue without questioning the other person's motives or personal worth.

Next, be very clear about your agreements. If you are having misunderstandings, take time to write out what you intend to do and how you'll communicate about progress along the way. Do this at the start. Be candid about what's realistic, what you can and can't do, and how you'll deal with uncertainties. Such actions build trust and produce successful results.

Finally, take part in outside activities with the people with whom you are building trust. Take field trips, share a meal, or find other ways to become better acquainted. The leader of a feuding group took his colleagues on a backcountry ride to see key project sites. "After ten hours bouncing around in a Bronco together," he explained, "barriers came down."

Identify those with whom you need to develop a stronger level of trust in your business or organization. Schedule the time and take the steps to fulfill this important priority.

Trust in the Ten-Step Process

Being able to truly trust another person takes time. In fast-changing environments, you may have little time to reach desirable levels of personal trust. Trusting in and adhering to the ten-step process provides a critically important bridge. Members of a business or community group may not trust or even know the other participants, but they can trust the ten-step process to enable them to get results together.

The process addresses the factors that erode people's trust. It eliminates disrespectful and personal attacks, partisan agendas, and fuzzy agreements that lack commitment. It invites honesty, respect for other points of view, and a commitment to shared hopes. The ten-step process involves everyone and enables them to learn from one another. It also builds the consistency and confidence that trust requires. The techniques outlined in this chapter can be implemented immediately to dissolve old differences. As you go through the process, you will build trust along the way.

BE AN AGENT OF HOPE

Many opportunities exist to dissolve long-standing differences. Rather than "working" on the problems, which often just heightens the irritation, like rubbing salt in an open wound, look for creative and playful ways to change the dynamics and help participants recognize new possibilities.

The clues to the Balance Nails game are: (1) Create alignment; (2) Balance your heads; (3) Reinforce alignment; (4) Think 3-D.

EPILOGUE:

Be an Agent of Hope in a Fearful World

This book is filled with steps, strategies, and stories that will help your group face tough issues and produce great results, but the most important part of the process is *you.* How will you choose to respond to the opportunities? Will you allow yourself to get caught up in the fear-filled dynamics of divisive debates, or will you free your hopeful self? These are simple questions, but the answers can be difficult.

In the heat of the moment, under pressure to perform, all of us can revert to the self-protective measures hardwired into our psyches. Occasionally, threats to life and core interests warrant the adrenaline rush of the fight-or-flight response. But, more often, circumstances don't require something that drastic.

MAKE THE RIGHT CHOICE TO MAKE A BIG DIFFERENCE

People and situations push our buttons every day. But we can choose individually and collectively to escape from that trap.

It is up to you to recognize the signs within yourself and your colleagues that fear-filled dynamics are at work in your organization. You can choose the ten-step process and the obstacle-overcoming strategies outlined in this book to realize great results that support the hopes you share. Your choice will make a big difference to your organization's bottom line and to your personal well-being.

Fear and greed frequently prompt people to try to control outcomes in order to satisfy their preformed objectives. A self-centered approach like this can distract a group from recognizing new opportunities that can benefit everyone in more fulfilling ways.

Central to the ability to make good decisions on difficult issues is the need to let go of your expectations and personal agenda. In her highly acclaimed book, *Leadership and the New Science—Learning about Organization from an Orderly Universe* (Berrett-Koehler, 1992), Meg Wheatley finds encouragement for relaxing the desire to control outcomes. She writes, "In many [physical] systems, scientists now understand that order and conformity and shape are created not by complex controls, but by the presence of a few guiding formulae or principles." Similarly, human organizations can use the positive spirit alive within them to guide their work in more natural and fulfilling ways.

PURSUE YOUR HOPES IN EVEN THE DARKEST MOMENTS

Hopes aren't luxuries that are restricted to the good times. They are bright beacons that can guide you through the darkest nights you face.

The situation confronting Bob, chief financial officer for a California-based organization, is a case in point. Hammered by California's worst recession in decades, Bob's firm faced huge budget cutbacks. Bob needed to eliminate $5 million to $7 million from an already lean $50 million budget. With increases in critical fixed costs, the real gap was even larger. Trimming fat alone wouldn't fix it. The organization needed to cut into muscle to do the job, and it would hurt.

Fears among employees and board members ran high as they wondered what projects would get cut and which people would lose their jobs. Why couldn't someone solve the problem? Without positive leadership, people in the organization might have taken out their frustrations on one another. Working within the fear-filled dynamics of divisive debate, they would have exacerbated the very scarcity they feared.

Other financial managers might have dodged the real issues by making proposals for across-the-board cuts and the like, but Bob remained hopeful. Even in this atmosphere of the gloom and with intense pressure on him to balance the budget, Bob encouraged others in the organization to be their better selves and pursue their shared hopes. "Especially in this time of crisis," he told the board and management team, "we need to focus on what we hope to accomplish, on what's most important. With more than $40 million remaining in the budget, we can even pursue new initiatives. We have choices, and we can get through this together." Bob wasn't being a Pollyanna. He was being keenly practical. In the face of mounting fears, he opted for hopes and invited everyone to work together.

Bob's choice in the way he responded and led others made a difference. The board followed the principles and practices of the ten-step process and established clear priorities. Instead of focusing on what would have to be cut, they targeted what they wanted to happen. The cuts in other areas tore into some of the muscle in the organization; nevertheless, the team managed to preserve the heart of its business—what was really most important to accomplish. Although making budget cuts is never easy, this approach brought people together to make them, with a larger sense of purpose to guide them.

TURN MERCHANTS OF FEAR INTO AGENTS OF HOPE

As you've seen from the examples in this book, basing your problem-solving approach on shared hopes supplies you with extraordinary power to resolve tough issues and achieve the results you are seeking. The steps outlined in this book, as well as the principles behind them, can also help you see situations in a new light and make even good things better.

For example, the leaders of a select group of highly successful law firms around the country wanted to enhance their practices. "We'd like to find out how to take our firms to the next level," they explained. "We have excellent clients and good incomes. How can we do even better and enjoy it more?"

A barrier to building a stronger practice is the way people regard attorneys—frequently with wariness. As a friend says, "Attorneys have a PR problem. People need them for certain things, but basically they don't want to use them any more than necessary." Perhaps unwittingly, some attorneys function as merchants of fear, who continually issue warnings about everything that might go wrong.

Fear is an effective hook for capturing people's attention and sometimes even for selling them something. Most marketers' toolkits pander to fear, greed, and envy, no matter what they sell. The trouble with fear as a tool or motivator is that once the threat subsides, people flee because the energy generated by fear isn't self-sustaining. Someone has to keep whipping up the frenzy of potentially dire consequences to keep it going. Without that constant churning, people eventually grow weary of fear tactics and withdraw without having addressed their problems.

Given this preexisting dynamic, what could these law firms do to enhance and sustain their relationships with clients? They found their solution when they examined the dynamics of hope and fear. They performed the exercise at the end of Part 1 of this book and wrote out their descriptions of what they thought, how they felt, how they acted, and what their relationships with others were like when they operated from a position of hope. They contrasted these responses with their reactions when they operated out of fear.

Having acquired insight into their own behavior, the leaders of this group of law firms turned to considering experiences from their clients' perspectives. In what state of mind did clients show up at their offices? Fearful. In what state should they leave in order to maintain a self-sustaining client-firm relationship? Hopeful.

These lawyers went back to their firms and involved everyone from receptionists to attorneys in an examination of their interactions with clients both in person and through written materials. They targeted how they could help each client shift from fear to hope. As a result, they revised their marketing materials, reoriented their client interviews, and established new objectives. As one lawyer remarked, "This perspective gives us a whole new way to look at our work and serve our clients. It's a positive approach for us to grow our practice and our profitability and know that we are responding to our clients' deepest needs and aspirations."

Likewise, you can apply these hopes-based principles and practices to bring new life to your own business or organization. Locate the areas where fears are undermining your efforts. Then pursue your hopes and those of your customers, coworkers, and community members to attract ideas, energy, and support for effective decision making and the productive future that can result.

PERSONAL PRINCIPLES

The following principles guide my own use of the ten-step process. It's taken me a long time in my journey to learn them, value them, and apply them. You don't need to believe them to follow the process and get good results. I offer them because I have found them helpful and perhaps you will, too.

1. *Each of us is valued and valuable.* The creative spirit alive within us loves each person fully, passionately, and unconditionally. No one is inherently more worthy than anyone else. Therefore, we are to honor and respect each person. We are not to put down or devalue anyone. Everyone who has a stake in a decision can participate in a way that reflects her or his inherent value. While we each have preferences, no person has preferential status.

2. *Each of us is free to change.* We do not need to score points with one another, defend past positions, or otherwise prove our worthiness. Similarly, we don't need to explain why we approached decisions the way we did in the past or worry about losing face to change what we are doing now.

3. *Life is abundant.* Even amid physical scarcity and deprivation, we can live abundantly—we can be fully alive to the mysteries and joys of life. We may not get what we want, but we can get what we need—the opportunity to exercise our talents, be respected and valued, and appreciate the wonder of life itself. The universe is a friendly place full of creative possibilities if we are willing to live in harmony with it rather than impose our own wills upon it.

4. *Hopes, not fears and expectations, can guide us.* Hopes attract and unleash positive, enduring energy. In contrast, fears and expectations offer a quick adrenaline rush but then diminish and drain energy. Hopes are not bound by current "realities"—they transcend them.

5. *We don't have to do all the work.* Traditional views of the rugged, self-reliant individual feed our egos and our desire for self-importance and control. But they do not fit with the interdependent world in which we live. Further, many people find help from their religious beliefs and seek guidance through reflection and prayer.

6. *Cooperation, not competition, wins.* Glorifying competition and conflict denies our shared humanity. "Survival of the fittest," "ruthless competition," and other supposedly Darwinian notions rampant in our social and business structures fail to reflect that cooperation is our highest calling. Cooperation with one another and with the deeper spirit within us is our best avenue for growth and fulfillment. Contrary to a common cultural assumption, conflict is not necessary.

Whether you believe in and follow these principles or choose others (or choose no formal set of principles), I encourage you to experiment with the ten-step process. See what works for you and your group and discover the many benefits the process offers. If you follow its straightforward steps, it will positively change both your outlook and your way of working with others. It will help you make great decisions.

BE WISE AS A SERPENT AND INNOCENT AS A DOVE

Being an agent of hope is not for the faint of heart. The biblical advice to be "as wise as a serpent and as innocent as a dove" is as valid today as it was 2,000 years ago. This advice is reflected in the dual nature of the ten-step process, which both welcomes and includes all participants and their shared hopes, while simultaneously honoring and protecting them from pitfalls and potential abuse as they resolve tough issues together.

The ten-step process can be compared to a well-designed aircraft that soars and safely transports its passengers to distant destinations. This process will help you and the people with whom you are working to resolve even the toughest issues in your organization and to get where you want to go—and then go even further.

I encourage you to be an agent of hope in a fearful world hungering for fresh solutions. Enjoy the flight!

APPENDIX A

The Ten-Step Improvement Checklist

As the steps and examples throughout this book have illustrated, you can make immediate changes in the way you approach tough issues to get great results. The following information will help you to quickly assess your starting point, compare your situation with that of others, target key improvements, and track your progress.

ASSESSING YOUR CURRENT PRACTICES

The following questionnaire measures how well your group or organization is currently aligned with the ten-step process. Each statement reflects one element of effective team decision making, and the score you give it will reveal how your organization now approaches important decisions.

Score each statement with a number between 0 and 10:

0 = never 5 = sometimes 10 = always

1. *We involve all people who have a stake in or knowledge about the topic.*

   Many groups falter at the first step. People who have knowledge about or a stake in the results get left out, and the organization loses good ideas. People who are left out of the process resist implementing the decision. To what extent are you involving everyone who should be involved or may have useful information?

2. *We expressly state our hopes for the organization and specific hopes for each major project or decision.*

   If you aren't clear about where you want to go, you won't get there. You need a set of guiding objectives with which participants can align themselves. Hopes are very different from a preexisting attachment to a specific outcome. Do you consistently express your aspirations and why they are important to you?

3. *We listen to each person's thoughts and feelings about a topic to understand the real issue(s).*

   Too many organizations start to solve a problem or decide on a course of action before they understand the real issue(s). Does your team listen carefully and respectfully to each person's perceptions? It pays off in greater clarity and a deeper level of buy-in from participants.

4. *All the options for a project or decision get out on the table.*

   Does your organization air all of the alternatives before leaping to a conclusion? Or do participants come to the discussion with preset ideas to advocate? Superior performers search out a wide range of possible solutions before drilling down on a particular one.

5. *We focus our information gathering on how the options help us realize our hopes.*

   Does the information you gather link to the shared hopes you want to pursue? Do participants see this as a way to learn together, or do they focus on gathering support for their own positions?

6. *When we review our choices, we listen to everyone's negatives and positives on each option before deciding.*

   Does everyone express something negative and something positive about each option? Or do participants stake out positions they want to advocate or defend? Ego attachment to particular points of view kills effective team decision making.

7. *Each person expresses her or his candid judgment on which choices would best advance the team's hopes.*

   Do you get each person's unbiased view of what would be best for the organization? Can participants register their choices with secret straw ballots without pressure to conform or fear of losing face if they have changed their minds? Or do certain people dominate the decision process or cause others to be uncomfortable about expressing their views?

8. *We summarize the individual conclusions and identify the most desirable course of action as well as other acceptable choices.*

   Do participants work together to improve what appears to be the most favored choice by considering elements of other favored choices? Do you come up with only one solution, or do you also identify acceptable alternative solutions to deal with changes that might occur later?

9. *We monitor whether our decisions are working and promptly modify them as needed.*

   Do you set a specific time frame in which to assess how well your decision is working? Is this checkpoint less than halfway to the time when the situation might change and require a new direction? Do your decisions keep up with the pace of change?

10. *We celebrate the team's progress and the fulfillment of our hopes.*

    Is your decision process joyful? Do you recognize and celebrate how your choices help your organization fulfill its objectives?

After you score each statement, add up your scores from each of the ten steps to determine your Ten-Step Quotient (TQ). If your score is 90 or more, your group demonstrates outstanding teamwork and the capacity to reach and implement effective decisions. If your score is between 60 and 90, your team has many strengths on which to build and opportunities for growth. An initial score between 40 and 60 is typical of many groups. Most organizations haven't discovered and consistently applied these proven steps for reaching great decisions. Below 40, your group is drastically underusing the talents of its members. They are probably locked into very limiting decision-making dynamics and need to make major changes immediately.

Whatever your TQ score is, you can boost it quickly by following the principles and practices of the ten-step process. This advantage of the process stands in contrast to other assessment scores, such as intelligence quotient (IQ) or emotional intelligence (EQ), which are difficult to improve individually or collectively. Changing fundamental personal traits is typically a long, gut-wrenching endeavor; however, changing the process people follow is much quicker and easier. With a commitment to change and to follow the steps outlined in this book, your team can rapidly improve its performance.

COMPARING YOUR ASSESSMENT WITH OTHERS

The assessment checklist provides an easy way to initiate a discussion about your group's practices with its members. Compare how members scored individual steps. Ask everyone if they agree on the assessment and what they consider to be its significance. Participants don't always have a clear perspective on behaviors that limit their team's performance. A group self-assessment will hold up a mirror so that everyone can see.

When discussing the assessment, ask the following questions:

1. *Where are our key opportunities for improvement?* Discuss how the gaps between your group's current practices and those of

the ten-step process limit your results or cause frustration. This discussion is even more important than your specific scores. Focus on how your current practices affect your results, then consider how the ten-step process can yield the most improvement for your group.

2. *How do your scores compare with those of other organizations?* You can compare your group's scores on individual steps with the results from thirty-six organizations that assessed themselves before learning and applying the ten-step process. The survey included middle managers in a wide range of organizations: manufacturing firms, service businesses, and government and educational organizations of various sizes. I focused on middle managers because they generally exhibit a healthy level of candor and are in a position to see up, down, and sideways in their organizations. The questions asked respondents to what degree their organizations already employed practices like those in the ten-step process (following the preceding self-assessment questionnaire).

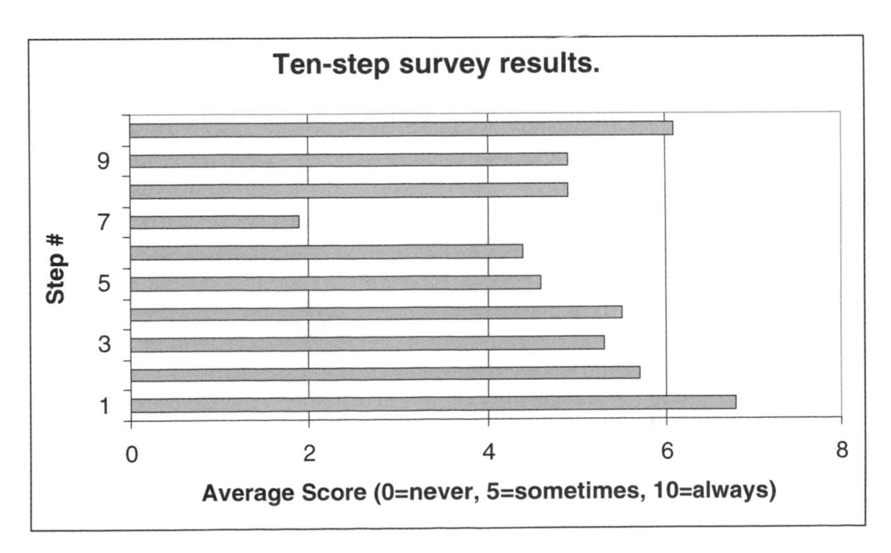

FIGURE 19 Ten-step survey results.

When scoring the individual steps, some respondents reported scores as low as 0 or 1, while a few scored some as high as 9 or 10. Figure 19 summarizes the average score for each of the ten steps, revealing major gaps between typical organizational practices and the elements of the ten-step process.

The sums of the scores on the ten steps (TQs) for respondents ranged from a low of 22 to a high of 91 out of 100. The average was 50. Fewer than 10 percent reported significant use (a TQ score of 76 or higher) of practices similar to the ten-step process. (See Figure 20.) So while some organizations have a few of the ingredients, very few have discovered and put the full recipe to use.

The TQ scores correlated closely with the respondents' assessments of their organization's performance. Those firms that more frequently and more extensively applied ten-step practices reported better success in realizing great results. (See Figure 21.) Firms with higher TQ scores also reported better use of participants' potential and more learning. You can take the survey online and compare your results with other organizations at this book's Web site, www.howgreatdecisionsgetmade.com.

A low TQ score is not a badge of failure—it's an opportunity for substantial improvement. By closely following the ten-step process,

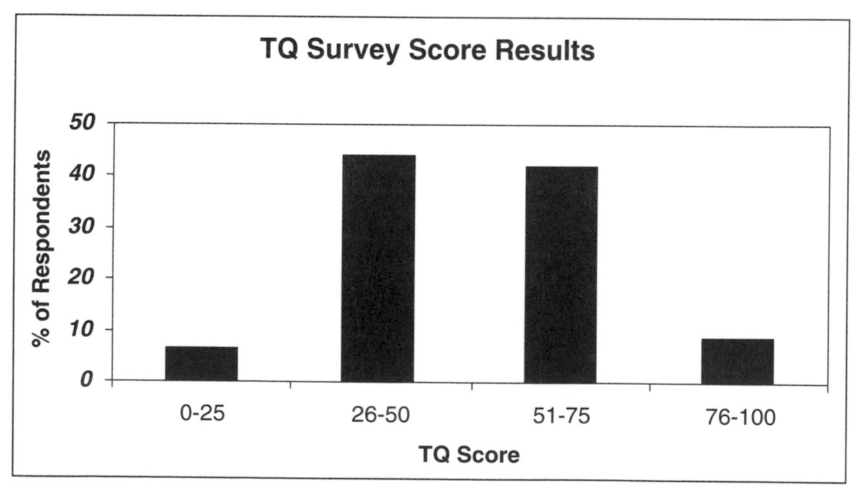

FIGURE 20 TQ survey score results.

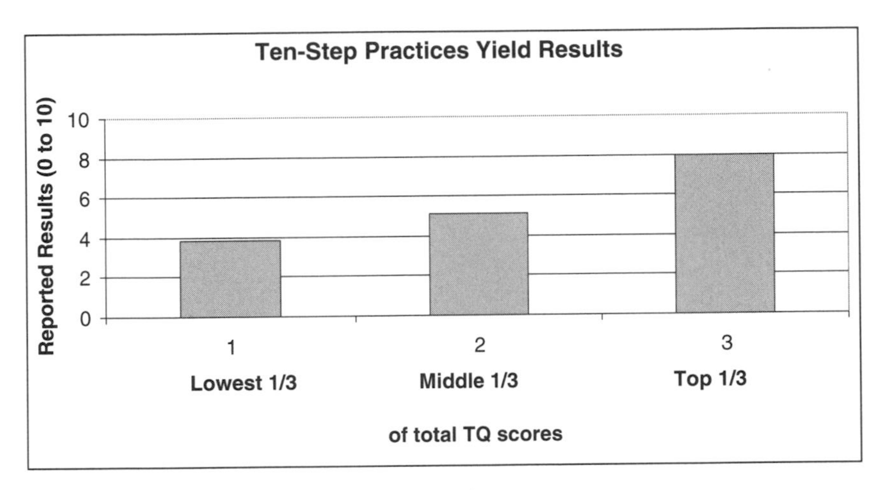

FIGURE 21 Ten-step practices yield results.

every business or organization can readily increase its score and produce significant and lasting results.

TARGETING YOUR IMPROVEMENTS AND TRACKING YOUR RESULTS

Once you have a sense of where your business or organization stands, you need to decide what you're going to do. Making assumptions about what will and won't work in your group will limit your use of the ten-step process.

The best way to proceed is to develop a plan for learning and applying the process. Pick a tough issue you'd like to resolve and commit to using the ten-step process. Set up a time three or six months later to repeat the assessment checklist and see how well you're doing. If you stick with the process, your progress will amaze you.

Bibliography

The following is a short list of books and articles that I have found personally valuable. It is not intended to be exhaustive. Instead, it guides you to specific resources and highlights why I've found these resources to be useful. All references are to currently available editions.

LISTENING EFFECTIVELY

Rogers, Carl. *The Carl Rogers Reader* (Mariner, 1989) and *A Way of Being* (Mariner, 1995). These books include discussions of reflective listening techniques. Reflective listening was one of the core skills taught in my class on negotiation and intervention at Stanford Business School more than twenty years ago. It remains one of the most powerful tools for discerning real issues and guiding others to find solutions.

Wheatley, Margaret J. *Turning to One Another: Simple Conversations to Restore Hope to the Future* (Berrett-Koehler, 2002). This thoughtful book invites us to start listening to one another again as an important step toward resolving issues. It offers a series of conversation starters to help readers explore their deepest aspirations and to reclaim conversation as our route back to one another.

STIMULATING CREATIVITY

Bryan, Mark, Julia Cameron, and Catherine Allen. *The Artist's Way at Work: Riding the Dragon* (Quill, 1999). This book offers daily practices, such as the valuable "morning pages," to sort through thoughts and feelings, develop focus, and identify key actions.

Gawain, Shakti. *Creative Visualization: Use the Power of Your Imagination to Create What You Want in Your Life* (New World Library, 2002). This book helps bring creativity into focus. The openness to letting better results than our personal agendas come forth is especially compelling.

Ray, Michael, and Rochelle Myers. *Creativity in Business* (Doubleday, 1986). This is a classic on bringing creativity to work. The practices discussed here have stood the test of time and remain valuable guidance for finding innovative solutions.

von Oech, Roger. *A Kick in the Seat of the Pants—Using Your Explorer, Artist, Judge, & Warrior to Be More Creative* (Harper & Row, 1986). This book suggests practical and fun ways to stimulate new ideas. The trigger concept tool demonstrates that everyone has innovative ideas just waiting to take form.

FACILITATING GROUPS

Doyle, Michael, and David Straus. *How to Make Meetings Work* (Berkeley Publishing, 1993). This book gives practical guidance on how to structure and guide meetings.

Kaner, Sam. *Facilitator's Guide to Participatory Decision-Making* (New Society Publishers, 1996). This book outlines useful ways to think about decision making in groups. The "gradients of agreement" discussion is particularly helpful for guiding groups to recognize a spectrum of choices.

PROVIDING LEADERSHIP

Collins, Jim. *Good to Great—Why Some Companies Make the Leap . . . and Others Don't* (Harper Business, 2001). This book explores the inner chemistry of how companies can become great.

Perkins, Dennis N. T. *Leading at the Edge* (AMACOM, 2000). This account of Shackleton's Antarctic exploration offers an engaging metaphor of leadership as an expedition.

Peterson, Eugene. *The Message—The Bible in Contemporary English* (Navpress, 2002). This is a highly readable way to access timeless wisdom. Commentators observe that in hundreds of places in the Old and New Testaments the scriptures advise not to be afraid.

Wheatley, Margaret. *Leadership and the New Science: Discovering Order in a Chaotic World Second Edition* (Berrett-Koehler, 1999). This book demonstrates the inherent orderliness of the universe and encourages organizations to follow self-organizing principles in their activities.

EXPLORING SPIRITUAL TRADITIONS OF DECISION MAKING

St. Ignatius Loyola, *The Spiritual Exercises of Saint Ignatius,* translated by Thomas Corbishley, S. J., (Anthony Clarke, 1973). These exercises include the rules for spiritual discernment that underlie the decision-making process Art Stevens outlined for me. The rules tap three elements: reasoning, emotions, and the guidance of a greater spirit.

Bots, Jan, S. J. "Praying in Two Directions: A Christian Method of Prayerful Decision-making," *Review for Religious,* Jan–Feb, 1982. This article discusses the concept of "holy indifference." It is a willingness to let the best result come forward even if it isn't what we expected or how we personally wanted it to be. It inspires Step #2's focus on inviting participants to openly explore their deepest aspirations together.

Morneau, Robert F. "Principles of Discernment," *Review for Religious,* March–April, 1982. This article counsels patience to wait freely for a decision. Such patience allows fear-filled rushes of emotion or other pressures to subside during the decision-making process.

Schemel, George, S. J., and Sister Judith Roemer. "Communal Discernment," *Review for Religious,* Nov–Dec, 1981. This article suggests starting with the negatives about an option and exchanging information without debate (Step #6). Participants may not be of one mind about a particular choice, but they can be of one spirit concerning the direction they choose.

Smith, Herbert F., S. J. "Discernment of Spirits," *Review for Religious,* vol. 35, 1976. Smith encourages prayer or meditation—the open, reflective opportunity to hear and respond to the positive, creative spirit within us. He underscores praying for alignment with the greater good rather than divine blessing for our personal agenda.

Index

About the Author

Don Maruska writes, speaks, and consults on successful decision-making steps. His work guides clients through such critical issues as new products for Fortune 500 companies, million-dollar-a-day manufacturing problems, obstacles stalling fast-growth businesses, multi-million-dollar budget deficits facing government agencies, and controversies over natural resources.

Don has more than thirty years' experience building and growing organizations. He was vice president of marketing for the company that became E*Trade and was founder and CEO of three Silicon Valley companies, winning the National Innovators Award in 1988. As a venture investor, Don aided start-ups that became public companies. Earlier in his career, he served as a legislative advisor in the U.S. Senate and developed management procedures to implement a nationwide rental housing program. He also led consulting projects for McKinsey & Company. Don writes the "Business Success" column distributed through the Knight-Ridder Business Wire to more than 200 newspapers in the United States and through Reuters overseas.

Don Maruska's training includes an AB from Harvard University and an MBA and a JD from Stanford University. He lives with his wife and daughter on the shore of Morro Bay, California.

Don welcomes your reactions to this book and inquiries about situations in which you'd like to apply the decision process. You may contact the author at:

Don Maruska & Company, Inc.
895 Napa Avenue, Suite A-5
Morro Bay, California 93442
805-772-4667; 805-772-4697 (fax)
www.donmaruska.com or connect@donmaruska.com